Old Testament Essentials

CREATION, CONQUEST, EXILE AND RETURN

Tremper Longman III

IVP Connect

An imprint of InterVarsity Press
Downers Grove, Illinois

InterVarsity Press
P.O. Box 1400, Downers Grove, IL 60515-1426
World Wide Web: www.ivpress.com
E-mail: email@ivpress.com

InterVarsity Press® is the book-publishing division of InterVarsity Christian Fellowship/USA®, a movement of students and faculty active on campus at hundreds of universities, colleges and schools of nursing in the United States of America, and a member movement of the International Fellowship of Evangelical Students. For information about local and regional activities, write Public Relations Dept., InterVarsity Christian Fellowship/USA, 6400 Schroeder Rd., P.O. Box 7895, Madison, WI 53707-7895, or visit the IVCF website at <www.intervarsity.org>.

All Scripture quotations, unless otherwise indicated, are taken from the Holy Bible, New International Version®, NIV® Copyright © 1973, 1978, 1984, 2010 by Biblica, Inc.™ Used by permission. All rights reserved worldwide.

While all stories in this book are true, some names and identifying information in this book have been changed to protect the privacy of the individuals involved.

Cover design: Cindy Kiple
Interior design: Beth Hagenberg
Images: © james steidl/iStockphoto

ISBN 978-0-8308-1051-2 (print)
ISBN 978-0-8308-7194-0 (digital)

Printed in the United States of America ∞

Library of Congress Cataloging-in-Publication Data
A catalog record for this book is available from the Library of Congress.

P	23	22	21	20	19	18	17	16	15	14	13	12	11	10	9	8	7	6	5	4	3	2
Y	34	33	32	31	30	29	28	27	26	25	24	23	22	21	20	19	18	17				

To Alice

Contents

Preface

Christians love the Bible, but they often do not know what to do with the Old Testament. First, it is simply long (it composes about 77 percent of the Bible), and thus it is often hard to keep the basic plot of the Old Testament in mind. Further, it comprises many different types of writing, not just historical books. Indeed, the historical books (Genesis–Esther) contain genres other than simply narrative, for instance, law. Besides the historical books, the Old Testament contains prophecy (Isaiah, Jeremiah, Ezekiel and the twelve Minor Prophets), poetry (Psalms, Lamentations and Song of Songs), wisdom literature (Proverbs, Job and Ecclesiastes) and apocalyptic (Daniel). Each of these types of literature calls for a different reading strategy. In addition, parts of the Old Testament seem not only strange but embarrassing. Take, for instance, the wars of the book of Joshua, where God calls on the Israelites to kill every man, woman and child in Canaan, or the curses of the psalms, when the psalmist calls on God to injure and kill not only his enemies but his enemies' children. What are Christians supposed to do with these parts of sacred Scripture? And finally, Christians rightly focus their attention on Jesus Christ, their Lord and Savior. But one looks in vain for the name of Jesus in the pages of the Old Testament. Isn't it better to spend our time reading the New Testament?

Of course, the answer is no. The whole Bible, not just the New Testament, is Scripture and thus authoritative to Christian life and belief. Jesus himself made a point to tell his disciples that the whole Old Testament anticipated his coming (see especially Luke 24:25-27, 44-45). The study of the Old Testament is not easy since it is distanced from us in terms of culture, time and redemptive history (that is, it was written before the fuller revelation of Christ), but it is worth the effort in terms of knowing God and knowing how we are to live our lives in a manner that is pleasing to him.

It is with that spirit that I wrote Old Testament Essentials. The Bible readings, study questions and essays that make up the following seventeen studies serve three major purposes: (1) to acquaint you with the message of the Old Testament, (2) to show you how the Old Testament points to Jesus, and (3) to show you how the Old Testament is relevant to your life. It is my hope that your use of this guide will not only enrich your knowledge of the content of the Old Testament but also deepen your love of the Old Testament, and of the One who speaks through its pages to you.

I would like to thank Cindy Bunch of InterVarsity Press for the invitation to write this volume as well as Drew Blankman who gave me excellent advice as I brought it to its final form. In addition, my good friend Ray Aromatorio used this guide in manuscript form in a Bible study he leads. He and the members of the group gave me great advice. Ray is a constant source of encouragement and support to me. Of course, any errors in the final product are my own. I would also like to thank my wife for her love for and forbearance of me over the forty years of our marriage (we celebrated it on June 23, 2013). I decided to become a professor and writer under her influence. Little did she know that she would create a monster, though my mother did warn her that "I do things to death." I love you, honey.

Tremper Longman III

Introduction
How to Use This Book

Having taught for over thirty years, I know the struggle that many Christians have with the Old Testament. In the first place, the Old Testament is long, constituting over three-quarters of the Bible. Second, much of it seems strange and distant from us today. There are customs that are foreign to our experience (for example, sacrifices) and features that are deeply off-putting if not repulsive (for example, holy war).

Thus, we have a tendency to stay in the New Testament. After all, we reason, we find Jesus Christ in the New Testament, and he is undoubtedly the center of our faith. He is the one who died on the cross and was raised from the dead to save us from our sins. We don't need the Old Testament any more as long as we have Jesus.

However, the Christian church through the ages has recognized that God still speaks powerfully to us through the Old Testament. On occasion some church leaders have tried to make the argument that the Old Testament is no longer relevant and should be removed from the canon. A preacher named Marcion made the strongest case for this during the second century A.D. He believed that the Old Testament with its God of wrath was out of harmony with the New Testament and its presentation of Jesus as a God of love.

While his viewpoint became very popular, he was soon excommunicated for these views (in A.D. 144) because the broader church recognized that the Old Testament indeed was God's word to humanity. After all, Jesus himself was a student of the Old Testament, and much of the New Testament rests on the Old Testament as its foundation.

That is not to say that the Old Testament should be read and applied in exactly the same way it was before the coming of Christ. Just to choose one obvious example, Christians do not offer animal sacrifices anymore. But does that make the laws concerning sacrifice in the Old Testament irrelevant (Leviticus 1–7)? No. After all, the theological significance of Christ's death on the cross can only be understood on the background of the sacrificial system of the Old Testament (see Hebrews 10:1-18).

Furthermore, Jesus himself told his disciples in no uncertain terms that the Old Testament anticipated his coming. After his resurrection, Jesus berated his disciples for being "slow to believe all that the prophets have spoken" (Luke 24:25). He then goes on to explain how "all the Scriptures" (meaning the Old Testament) pointed to him (Luke 24:26-27, 45-48).

The purpose of this guide is to help you grasp the message of the Old Testament as it narrates God's work from the time of creation up to Israel's return from Babylonian exile. We will also look at Old Testament law, ritual practices (priests, holy places and sacrifices), wisdom and praise literature, as well as the prophets. The guide will not only help you grasp the contents of the Old Testament but also teach the best way to interpret the various parts of the Old Testament.

The guide is divided into seventeen studies, each having the same structure.

Bible Study—The heart of the study is reading the Scripture itself. Thus we begin with a reading assignment (and a memory verse that captures a central theme). The reading assignment is typically a selection of passages from the topic under study. I will also suggest a longer reading assignment that covers the whole topic in the Bible. Perhaps most people will want to go through the book the first time only reading the selected passages and then go back again and read through the longer suggested reading.

After reading the assigned passage, questions follow that will help you to think about some of the crucial issues of the passage.

Reading—Each study includes an essay that covers the high points of the biblical texts under discussion. This essay is followed by more questions that hope to prod even further thinking about the biblical text.

The last two major sections of the study intend to get you to consider the Old Testament from a New Testament perspective as Jesus taught in Luke 24.

Anticipating the New Testament—This section in particular explores how Jesus is anticipated in the Old Testament. As St. Augustine said, "The New Testament is in the Old Testament concealed; the Old Testament is in the New Testament revealed."

The Ancient Story and Our Story—In the final major section we will look at the important implications this ancient text has for our lives today.

While it is my hope and prayer that this study will increase knowledge and understanding of the Old Testament, it is my deeper desire that this study will engender your love of this important portion of God's Word, leading to a lifetime study.

1 / Creation

MEMORY VERSE: Genesis 1:1-2
BIBLE STUDY: Genesis 1–2
READING: God Creates the Cosmos

 **Bible Study Guide**

After reading Genesis 1–2, spend some time reflecting on this passage with the following questions in mind before looking at the Reading.

1. Notice that there are two separate accounts of creation here (Genesis 1:1–2:4a and Genesis 2:4b-25). Please write a brief description of the similarities and differences between the two accounts. What is the main subject of each?

2. In Genesis 1:2, the earth is described as "formless and empty." How do you picture that in your imagination?

3. Fill in the following boxes with what God created on each of the six days. Do you notice any relationship between the boxes for days 1-3 and those for days 4-6?

DAY 1	DAY 2	DAY 3
DAY 4	DAY 5	DAY 6

4. The psalmist proclaimed:

> What are mere mortals that you should think about them,
> > human beings that you should care for them?
> Yet you made them only a little lower than God
> > and crowned them with glory and honor. (Psalm 8:4-5 NLT)

In the first creation account (Genesis 1:1–2:4a), what are the indicators that human beings are the high point of creation, "a little lower than God"?

How about in the second account (Genesis 2:4b-25)?

5. All six creation days are said to have an evening and a morning, but the sun, moon and stars are not created until the fourth day. How does this affect your understanding of the creation "days"?

6. Human beings are said to be created in God's image. Do your best to explain what it means to be created in the image of God.

7. What is the significance of Adam being created from the dust of the ground and the breath of God (Genesis 2:7)?

8. Why did God create Eve?

9. What is the significance of the fact that Adam and Eve were naked and felt no shame?

Reading: God Creates the Cosmos

"In the beginning God created the heavens and the earth" (Genesis 1:1). These opening words of the Bible are foundational and radical. Considered both in their ancient context and today, they are indeed earth-shaking and life-transforming.

After all, we are fascinated by stories of beginnings, and the creation story provides insight on some of the biggest questions we have. Who are we, and where did we come from? What is our place in this big universe? Were we made for a purpose? Why do we yearn for relationship? What is our connection with the rest of the universe? And then there are the biggest questions of all. What about God? Who is he, and can we have a relationship with him?

Let's first explore Genesis 1–2 in its ancient context. The biblical story of creation was written in the light of these ancient rival claims of creation, not in the light of modern scientific ideas.

There were many rival creation accounts at the time. Take, for instance, the Babylonian story *Enuma Elish*. In this story a god and a goddess are just there at the beginning. They are primordial, not created. Their names are Apsu, the god of the salt water, and Tiamat, the goddess of the fresh waters. The waters, in other words, were there at the beginning. This idea is also found among the Egyptians, who believed that the waters, represented by the god Nun, were there before anything else. In contrast Genesis teaches that God created the waters. At first there was nothing and then "the earth was formless and empty, darkness was over the surface of the deep, and the Spirit of God was hovering over the waters" (Genesis 1:2). From nothing to a watery mass to, after six days, an ordered and functional creation.

In the Babylonian account the ordered universe came about through conflict between the creator god and the god of the primordial waters. In the *Enuma Elish* the mingling of the waters of Tiamat and Apsu brought forth the next generation of gods. These gods disturbed the sleep of Tiamat and Apsu, and Apsu determined to kill his divine children. But before he could carry out his plan, Ea, the god of wisdom, discovered his plot and delivered a preemptive strike. This victory was short-lived, however, since Apsu's death enraged Tiamat, who was more formidable than Apsu. Ea knew he was no match for her, so he called for a hero to step forward to save the gods from Tiamat and her demonic horde, which was led by the chief demon, Qingu. Marduk volunteered for the dangerous task on condition that if he won, he would become the king of the gods. And he did indeed vanquish Tiamat and became the most important god of the Babylonians. The Canaanites had a similar picture of a conflict between the creator god Baal and the god of the waters, named Yam. In Canaan as well as Babylon, conflict introduces creation.

Back to the Babylonian story, Marduk then took Tiamat's body and split it in half "like a shellfish." With the upper half, the god made the heavens, and with the lower the oceans. He then pushed back the lower waters and gave them boundaries, and in this way land was created. After this, Marduk executed Qingu. After this, he took some clay from the ground and mixed it with Qingu's blood, thus creating human beings.

Those who first heard Genesis 1–2 would have had these rival accounts ringing in their ears when they read how their God, alone and not with other gods, created the world from nothing. The "formless and empty" earth represents the watery mass to be sure, but God did not by conflict turn that watery mass that he created from nothing into an ordered and functional earth, but by his divine decree over six days and then a final seventh on which he rested.

Again, it is important to read the Bible's depiction of creation against the background of its original setting rather than against modern scientific ideas, though the creation account will have implications for how we understand the science of origins.

The connection with the ancient Near East, however, is a reminder that we are not getting a literal description of how God created but rather an assertion of the statement that God, not the gods of Babylon, Egypt or Canaan, created creation. This understanding is also highlighted by the obviously figurative language used in Genesis 1–2. Let's begin with the days of creation. On first glance it appears that these are literal twenty-four-hour days. After all, right from day one they are described as having an "evening and morning." Closer examination, though, shows that the author of Genesis could not have thought of these days as literal days with literal evenings and mornings. After all, such days require a rising and setting sun, a moon as well as stars, and these are not created until the fourth day.

The depiction of the creation week is a literary presentation of the great truth that the biblical God, and no others, created creation. The days have an interesting structure in that the first three days describe the creation of realms that are filled by the inhabitants of those realms in the second set of three days.

DAY 1	DAY 2	DAY 3
light and darkness	sky and waters	land
DAY 4	**DAY 5**	**DAY 6**
sun, moon and stars	birds and fish	animals and human beings

A second example of the highly figurative nature of the description of creation in Genesis 1–2, as well as its interaction and critique of pagan notions of creation, is found in the account of the creation of Adam in Genesis 2:7, "the LORD God formed the man from the dust of the ground. He breathed the breath of life into the man's nostrils, and the man became a living person" (NLT). Remember that the *Enuma Elish* described the creation of humans from the ground and the blood of a demon god. It is no accident that there are similarities and differences between the Bible and the writings of the ancient Near East; writing like this was a way of denying the Babylonian account that gave such a low view of humanity as connected to the demonic and thus inherently evil. To be created from the breath of God, on the contrary, expresses a profound understanding of the dignity of humanity.

While Genesis 1–2 teaches us little about *how* God created creation, it wonderfully proclaims important foundational truths about God, ourselves and our relationship to God. Let's explore some of the leading ideas.

ABOUT GOD

God created creation. Everything that exists exists because of God; everything and everybody else are creatures totally dependent on God. We owe our very lives to God. And, in contrast to ancient Near Eastern ideas of the time, he did this alone by the power of his word and not in conflict or with the assistance of other gods. There is only one God who deserves the worship of his creatures.

The creation account introduces the God of the Bible as one who is both transcendent as well as immanent. That is, he is not a part of creation, which is something that he makes, looks at and pronounces "good." On the other hand, he is involved in creation. He does not make it and stay uninvolved. This differentiates the biblical God from many other reli-

gions: those that say he is other and not involved (deism), and those that say he is a part of creation (pantheism).

Reading Genesis 1–2 in the light of the religions of the ancient Near East also highlights something that to us seems unexceptional but to the people of the ancient Near East would have been shocking and radical. God is neither gendered nor sexual. All the gods of the ancient Near East were either male or female, had sexual relations and bore children. The fact that God is neither male nor female is indicated by the fact that both men and women are created in the "image of God" (more about this later).

In sum then, God is the sovereign, self-sufficient and supreme Creator of all things.

ABOUT HUMANITY

That God created Adam and Eve from whom all humanity descends indicates that everyone owes their life to God. The manner in which God created Adam and Eve inform us about who we are as human beings. The emphasis is on human dignity, especially when Genesis 1–2 is read with rival texts like the *Enuma Elish* in the background. The creation of Adam from the dust of the ground and the breath of God, rather than the blood of a demon God, speaks to the fact that humans, though creatures like the other animals, have a special relationship with God. Genesis 1 also announces that human beings, male and female, are created in the "image of God" (Genesis 1:27). While clearly indicating humanity's special place in God's creation, no precise definition is given of the meaning of this phrase. However, by studying the word *image* elsewhere in Scripture, we observe its use in connection with human kings who set up images of themselves around their kingdom to represent their power and authority. On analogy, then, human beings represent God's presence, power and authority in the world. We reflect God's glory like the moon reflects the light of the sun. These and other features of the creation accounts in Genesis 1–2 emphasize humanity's dignity as God's creatures.

As God's image bearers, human beings were also commissioned to "fill" and "subdue" the earth. They are to "rule over the fish in the sea and the birds in the sky and over every living creature that moves on the ground" (Genesis 1:28). While some have wrongly read this verse as permitting humans to run rampant over the creation for their own benefit, it really is a command to responsibly care for the rest of creation like good rulers should care for and promote the interests of their subjects.

The story of the creation of Eve speaks volumes about the nature of human beings, as well as the relationship between the genders. In the first place, notice God's remarkable statement that "it is not good for the man to be alone" (Genesis 2:18). Think about this. Adam is in a harmonious relationship with God and lives in Eden, whose very name means "abundance." What else does he need? Well, God understands that we need human relationship as well. So he creates Eve, who is a "helper

suitable for him" (Genesis 2:18). We should be very careful not to read the idea of subordination into the word *helper* here, since it is used elsewhere to refer to God who is the "helper" of his people. In another context this word could be translated "ally." They will be partners in the business and, after Genesis 3, the battle of life.

Notice how the description of her creation also emphasizes equality between Adam and Eve. He puts Adam in a deep sleep, takes something from his side, perhaps a rib, and creates Eve. That God took something from Adam's side, and not from his head or from his feet, is theologically and practically significant. She is neither superior to him or inferior, but his equal.

Eve's creation leads to the first marriage and a biblical definition of the institution of marriage. "That is why a man leaves his father and mother and is united to his wife, and they become one flesh" (Genesis 2:24). Marriage first involves "leaving" parents (note that Psalm 45:10 implies that a wife must leave her parents as well). *Leaving* means that the married couple no longer gives their primary loyalty to their parents but rather to each other. The next step is to "weave" (be united to) each other. This weaving of two lives takes place through common experiences and communication. Then, finally, marriage involves "cleaving" to each other, becoming one flesh in the act of sexual intercourse.

Marriage is not the only institution addressed in the creation narratives. Notice that work is not a consequence of the Fall but rather was to be a human activity even if humans were not sinners. The task was noble, to tend and guard the Garden. I will have more to say about this in study 2.

In addition, the creation texts establish the pattern of six days of work and then a sabbath rest. The commandment to observe the sabbath is grounded in the presentation of the creation as a week of seven days, and God rests on the seventh (Exodus 20:8-11).

Finally, note how the creation accounts end: "Now the man and his wife were both naked, but they felt no shame" (Genesis 2:25 NLT). This physical nakedness indicates that there are no barriers—physical, psychological, spiritual, emotional— between Adam and Eve. There is harmony in the Garden among humans because there is harmony with the Creator God.

Reading Study Guide

1. List the ways in which the biblical creation account is similar but different from the ancient Near Eastern accounts described in the essay.

2. Read through the creation accounts and identify all the ways that humanity's dignity is communicated, both those mentioned in the essay and others.

3. Genesis 1:28 informs humanity that they should "fill" the earth and "subdue it." They should also "rule" over all the other creatures. What kinds of practical examples can you give of the proper exercise of this divine command? What examples can you give of its abuse?

4. In the light of God's comment that it was not good for Adam to be alone, is it appropriate to tell lonely people that they have God and that's all they need? What advice should we give people who are lonely?

5. How does Genesis 1–2 describe the relationship between Adam and Eve? What does it teach about humanity and about gender relationships? What kind of impact should Adam and Eve's relationship have on how we interact with the "other gender"?

6. How does the biblical definition of marriage shape your understanding of marriage today? If you are married, how does it affect your understanding of your own marriage? If you are not married, how does it influence your anticipation of marriage?

7. What insight does Genesis 1–2 give to your idea of work? Describe your attitude toward work (if you are a student, consider your schoolwork).

8. Are there other important truths taught about God or humanity in Genesis 1–2 that are not brought out in the essay?

Anticipating the New Testament

John 1:1-5, Colossians 1:15-20 and Revelation 3:14 inform us that Jesus participated in the creation of the world. He is after all God. The trinitarian nature of God is not revealed in all its glory until the New Testament, so we have a clearer idea of the involvement of the Father, Son and Holy Spirit in creation. It is not that we can identify specific and different roles that the persons of the Trinity play, but as Christians, we understand that the God-head is our Creator. The Father, the Son and the Spirit created us. We owe him everything.

Sadly, as we will see in study 2, sin deeply mars God's creation and his creatures, particularly humans. Thus, it is particularly interesting that the New Testament uses the language of new creation (see Isaiah 65:17; 66:22) to describe the future after Christ's second coming: "Then I saw 'a new heaven and a new earth,' for the first heaven and the first earth had passed away" (Revelation 21:1). By speaking of a new creation of heaven and earth, the biblical author warns against the view that the cosmos as we know it will simply be destroyed. It will not be destroyed; it will be transformed.

And, according to Paul, God's transformation of the old to the new creation has already begun! According to 2 Corinthians 5:17 (see also Galatians 6:15), "if anyone is in Christ, the new creation has come: The old has gone, the new is here!"

1. How does the New Testament's trinitarian perspective on the creation of the world change your perspective?

2. What does it mean to be a new creature in Christ?

3. What would a new earth and a new heaven look like?

⬭ The Ancient Story and Our Story

Genesis 1–2 presents a story of foundations or origins, informing us of crucial information about the nature of God, humanity and the world we live in. The narrative takes us beyond what we can see and experience with our senses to inform us concerning the ultimate nature of reality. Thus, these two chapters shape our view of the world.

Here we learn that God is our Creator. Though the highly figurative language that describes creation does not actually tell us about the process of creation, we do learn that the world and humanity came about through the action of a personal being, not through some impersonal chance process. This God created us, and we are totally dependent on him for our lives. God is above creation, but he is involved with his creation. There is no one who is like this God who created everything else.

We also learn that human beings are the high point of creation. Though we are creatures like everything else, we occupy a special place in that creation as the only ones designated as created in the "image of God." Humanity, you, me and everyone, has special dignity in God's world. That, of course, has important ramifications for how we should treat each other. We reflect who God is; we reflect his glory. Everyone deserves to be treated with respect. In addition, we learn in these opening chapters that we were not created to be isolated individuals but are made for relationship, with God and with each other. Marriage holds a special place among the relationships between human beings as the most intimate of all. Genesis 2 makes it clear that marriage is God-ordained and that sexuality is a gift from God.

As human beings created in the image of God, we also learn that we are to take care of God's world. The creation story indicates that the material world is important. Though in the history of the church, and even in some quarters today, the goodness of creation is rejected and downplayed, Genesis 1–2 serves the important function of telling us that such a view is wrong and even dishonors God who made the world and pronounced it "good." We are to be stewards of this world.

Looking Ahead

Adam and Eve stand naked before each other and feel no shame. They have nothing to hide because they have a harmonious relationship with God. But the next chapter of the story will bring their wonderful situation to an end.

Going Deeper

Longman, Tremper, III, *How to Read Genesis*. Downers Grove, IL: InterVarsity Press, 2005.
Walton, John H. *Genesis*. NIV Application Commentary. Grand Rapids: Zondervan, 2001.

2 / Fall

MEMORY VERSE: Romans 5:17
BIBLE STUDY: Genesis 3
READING: Humanity Rebels Against the Creator

 **Bible Study Guide**

After reading Genesis 3, spend some time reflecting on this passage with the following questions in mind before looking at the Reading. (For maximum benefit read Genesis 3–11.)

1. The serpent makes a sudden appearance in Genesis 3:1. What do you think Adam and Eve's reaction would be to discover a creature that is speaking badly about God?

2. What prepares the reader for the serpent's appearance in the chapter?

   Serpents were a well-known symbol for evil in the ancient Near East. How would this affect those who read Genesis 3 during the Old Testament period?

3. Would either Adam and Eve or later Israel identify the serpent with the devil?

4. Why did God prohibit eating from the tree of the knowledge of good and evil?

What would eating from the tree represent?

5. Is there any way in which Adam's sin differed from Eve's?

Who was responsible?

6. What is the significance of the fact that the text reveals that Adam was "with her" (Genesis 3:6) as the serpent was talking with Eve?

7. How does Adam and Eve's sin relate to later humanity, including you?

8. In what areas does God choose to punish the man and the woman?

Why do you think God chose these particular punishments for the man and the woman?

9. God said that Adam would die when he ate of the tree of the knowledge of good and evil, yet he doesn't. Was God misleading Adam?

10. What is the significance of God giving clothes to Adam and Eve?

Reading: Humanity Rebels Against the Creator

Nothing prepares the reader for the first sentence of Genesis 3: "Now the serpent was more crafty than any of the wild animals the LORD God had made." After all, at the end of Genesis 2, everything was "good." Adam and Eve were living in harmony with God, with each other and with their environment. The appearance of a creature working to undermine the relationship between God and his human creatures is unexpected. Who or what is this serpent and where did he come from?

The Bible never explains the serpent's origins. Christians rightly identify the serpent with Satan because of the New Testament (Romans 16:20; Revelation 12:9), but it is doubtful that Adam and Eve would have done so, or even the author of Genesis. Since the walking serpent was a well-known ancient Near Eastern symbol of evil, the original audience of Genesis would have recognized the danger inherent in the appearance of this creature, but in the world of the story itself, Adam and Eve were likely dumbfounded.

The serpent's evil intentions are revealed in his provocative question to Eve, "Did God really say, 'You must not eat from any tree in the garden'?" (v. 1). The serpent here mocks God by suggesting that God gave no provision for food in the Garden. The woman takes the bait and rises up to defend God (she is the first apologist), by specifying that God prohibited only one food source, the fruit of the tree of the knowledge of good and evil. Thus she is not only the first defender of God but also the first legalist, since she insisted not only that God forbade eating from the tree but also touching it. Legalists add to God's law, and Eve here adds the idea that they are not allowed to touch the tree. Legalism makes God look ridiculous, along with preventing people from enjoying life.

The serpent responds (vv. 4-5) by denying Eve's contention that she and Adam would die if they transgressed God's commandment concerning the tree. He suggests that God has misled them in order to keep them from getting the knowledge of "good and evil." The serpent's response raises the question of what exactly is at issue in the divine prohibition. After all, Adam and Even know what is good and evil already. They know it is wrong to eat the fruit of the tree. In Hebrew the word *know* (*yada‘*) does not refer to an intellectual apprehension of a matter but rather experience. In Genesis 4:1 we read that Adam "knew" his wife, and as a result she became pregnant and gave birth to Seth. Obviously, here the verb does not mean that Adam knew his wife in an intellectual sense but rather in an experiential sense. In Genesis 3 knowing good and evil is more than knowing what is right and wrong; it refers to the ability to define what is right and wrong. By eating of the tree, Eve and Adam assert their right to define good and evil rather than submitting to God's judgments. Thus, the sin of eating of the tree is an assertion of moral autonomy. They reserve the right to say what is right and wrong.

And they do assert their independence from God by eating the fruit of the tree. The woman does so first, but then she hands the fruit to Adam, "who was with her" (v. 6), and he eats it. Indeed, while the woman was deceived (1 Timothy 2:14), the man was silent and failed in his charge to "take care" of the Garden (Genesis 2:15).

They both rebelled against God and experienced the consequences of their act immediately. Adam and Eve are immediately estranged. Whereas before they could stand naked in each other's presence and feel no shame, now they hurry to cover their nakedness, and, significantly, they hide from God.

When God confronts him, Adam shifts the blame to Eve, who then shifts the blame to the serpent (Genesis 3:12-13). God knows that all three are to blame, and thus he punishes the serpent, the woman and the man in turn.

First, the walking serpent must forever slither on the ground. The second half (v. 15) of the serpent's punishment has ramifications that reverberate throughout redemptive history. God announces that conflict will persist between the offspring of the woman and the serpent's offspring. In other words, those who follow God and those who follow evil will be at each other's throat. Genesis 4 will illustrate this battle as Cain kills Abel, followed by a description

of the evil line of Cain (Genesis 4:17-26) and the godly line of Seth (Genesis 5:1-32). And the division between the godly and the ungodly continues throughout the biblical history until it comes to a climax when the offspring of the woman will crush the head of the serpent (see later on in the New Testament).

The woman's punishment (Genesis 3:16) centers on her most important relationships. First, her pain in childbirth will intensify. Note that the verse presumes that there was (or would have been) pain in childbirth even if Eve had not rebelled. But she did sin and so her pain becomes nearly unbearable. However, it is not only the mother-child relationship that experiences pain but also her relationship with her husband, though the pain has a different nature. The husband-wife relationship will experience conflict. Most translations imply that while wives will (romantically) desire their husbands, the husbands will respond by ruling (oppressing) them. This interpretation misunderstands the nature of the woman's desire. The Hebrew word is a rare one, occurring next in Genesis 4:7 where sin "desires" Cain. Needless to say, sin does not desire romantic involvement with Cain but rather desires to dominate him. It is this sense of desire, that is, desire to control, which is operative in verse 16. Thus, the punishment of the woman describes the power play between the genders where each tries to dominate the other.

Finally, God punishes Adam, inflicting pain on his work. Remember that Adam was charged by God to work even before his rebellion. In Genesis 1:28, God told Adam to "subdue" the earth. He said to "rule over the fish of the sea and the birds in the sky and over every living creature that moves on the ground." Even more to the point, God told Adam to "work" in the Garden and "take care" of it (Genesis 2:15). He then created Eve to be his "helper" in this dignified work (Genesis 2:18). Thus work is not a result of sin, but the pervasive frustration that people experience in their work is the consequence. Humans will struggle in their work.

While it is tempting to think that God punishes women in their relationships and men in their work, because men and women have different roles, such a conclusion would be wrong. Men have important relationships in which they experience pain, and women work and feel the frustration of work. Perhaps, though, the focus of their respective punishment does point to what men and women find or at least tend to find most important. Whatever the case, these punishments are only the beginning of the pain that is introduced by Adam and Eve's rebellion.

After all, God announced that the punishment for breaking his command not to eat of the fruit of the tree of the knowledge of good and evil was death (Genesis 2:17). Now, granted, Adam and Eve did not drop dead the moment they ate the fruit, but death became inevitable the moment they transgressed the divine command. They were ejected from the Garden of Eden and removed from the tree of life.

While some people think of the tree of life as a magical tree believing that eating its fruit would automatically confer eternal life on a person, the truth lies in a different direction. Adam and Eve were eating from the tree of life while they were in the Garden. After all, it was only the fruit from the tree of the knowledge of good and evil that was prohibited. Thus, God's urgency in removing them from the Garden was to separate them from the tree of life and when this was accomplished, death was inevitable with time.

And ejected they were. God then placed cherubim with flaming swords at the entrance of Eden to block reentry. The cherubim are the most powerful of God's angelic host. Their presence with swords indicates the new level of hostility that has come into the cosmos. While before God moved against disorder to produce a functional universe with the energy of an artist, now God will restrain and ultimately defeat the disorder caused by evil with the power of a warrior with his army.

Thus, Adam and Eve sinned against God. God then announced their punishment and executed his judgment by removing them from the Garden. However, before actually punishing them God demonstrated his continuing care for them. He shows that he will stay involved with his rebellious people in spite of their sin. He does this by providing them with clothing. This clothing is a token of his grace toward his human creatures. He does not destroy or abandon them, but works toward their redemption.

What is the significance of the story of

Adam and Eve's rebellion against God? Why is this story told at this juncture in the biblical text? As Paul will later explain (Romans 5:12), the story tells of the moment that sin and death entered the world. It explains to its ancient and modern readers that the sinful and confused world they experience is not the result of God's creation but rather of human willfulness. From then on all of God's creatures will sin and die. It is not that Adam and Eve's sin is counted as our sin and that we died because they died. It is not a matter of genetics. It is rather that Adam and Eve, as our representatives, demonstrate what all of us would do if we were in that place. We are rebels against God, but thanks be to God that he does stay involved with us and work toward our redemption.

Thus, the chapter ends on a depressing note. At the conclusion of chapter 2, Adam and Eve stood naked and unashamed in each other's presence. Now, however, they must seek cover from each other. They can no longer stand completely vulnerable and open toward each other. Once again, this nakedness is not just physical but also psychological, emotional and spiritual. Sin creates estrangement from God and alienation from each other and from creation itself.

Reading Study Guide

1. While Eve was the first "apologist" for God in her interaction with the serpent, her engagement with the serpent resulted in disaster. What would have been a better response to the serpent's question?

   Are there any implications for how we should interact with those who critique Christianity today?

2. In response to the serpent, Eve says that God commanded them not to eat from the tree of the knowledge of good and evil, or even to touch it (Genesis 3:3). In the Reading, we observed that Eve added to the divine prohibition and was the first legalist.

What are some examples of legalism today?

What is the danger of legalism?

3. While Genesis 1–2 does not explicitly describe the introduction of evil in the world that would explain the serpent's behavior, some read a fall of Satan and demons in the space between the first two verses of Genesis. In other words, Genesis 1:1 describes the full-blown creation, while verse 2 describes the earth as "a formless void." This view goes by the name the "gap theory," because it reads a lot into the "gap" between the verses. What are the strengths and weaknesses of such a theory?

4. Read Isaiah 14:12-20. Some have considered this a remembrance of the fall of Satan, who then is identified with the serpent of Genesis 3. Read Isaiah 14:1-11 (in particular note v. 4). How does this context for verses 12-20 discourage the idea that they refer to the fall of Satan?

5. The Reading suggested that at the heart of the rebellion of Adam and Eve was an assertion of moral autonomy. Put in your own words what this means. Is it fair to say that all sin involves an assertion of moral autonomy? Give examples.

6. The Reading suggested that God chose to punish women in the area of relationship and men in the area of work not because men don't have relationships or women don't

work, but because women tend to put more value on relationships than men, and men tend to place more significance on their work than women. Discuss this point. Do you agree or not? Why?

7. Genesis 3 is a story of human sin. God responds to sin by announcing a judgment against them. Before the execution of judgment, God extends a token of his grace to show Adam and Eve that he remains involved with them. The three stories that follow Genesis 3 have the same basic four-part structure. Read the following passages and identify these four parts:

- Cain and Abel (Genesis 4:1-16)

- The flood story (Genesis 6–9)

- The tower of Babel (read Genesis 11:1-9 first, then Genesis 10)

8. What is Genesis 3–11 teaching us about God and human beings by presenting four accounts of human sin followed by divine judgment and grace?

⮂ Anticipating the New Testament

In Romans 8, Paul points out that the "creation was subjected to frustration" (Romans 8:20). Here he alludes to God's punishment of Adam and Eve in Genesis 3, which had dire ramifications not only for all human beings through time but also for the entire creation. But Paul does not stop there; he also looks forward to the time when "the creation itself will be liberated from its bondage to decay and brought into the freedom and glory of the children of God" (Romans 8:21).

In Romans 5:12-21 and 1 Corinthians 15:20-21, 44-49, he also reflects on the present sinful condition of humanity as well as our redemption by making a comparison between Adam and Christ. Adam was the first human, and he introduced sin and death into the world. He was the first to sin, and the consequence was death. Every human shares his disposition to sin, and sin so affects our world that it is not possible for us not to sin. We too deserve death because we have all sinned (see Romans 5:12).

However, if Adam was the one to introduce sin and death into the world, Jesus introduced righteousness and life to those who will receive the gift (Romans 5:15-19)! As Paul says in 1 Corinthians 15:22, "For as in Adam all die, so in Christ all will be made alive."

1. According to Paul, what was the consequence of Adam's transgression?

2. Paul draws a comparison between Adam and Jesus. In what ways are they alike?

3. He also notes differences between Adam and Jesus. Can you name them?

⬤ The Ancient Story and Our Story

In the previous study we learned that we, human beings, were created in the image of God and reflect the divine glory. Human dignity arises from the fact that God "made them only a little lower than God" (Psalm 8:5 NLT). In Genesis 1–2, we learn that humanity lives in harmony with God and with each other, relationships are rich and work is satisfying.

This description, however, is largely out of keeping with the human condition as we experience it today, and Genesis 3 tells us why. The struggles that we presently experience in our relationships, with our world, with ourselves and with God are not the result of how God created us but rather because of our rebellion. The story of Adam and Eve eating from the tree of the knowledge of good and evil represents what we all do. We refuse to listen to God's commands and substitute our own moral judgments in place of his. As a result, we are broken and our world is fractured. Why are relationships hard? Why is work frustrating? Why do we let ourselves down? The answer, according to Genesis 3, is human sin.

Fortunately, the contribution of Genesis 3 does not end there. While we learn that God judges sin, we also see that God immediately pursues our redemption and reconciliation. He anticipates the destruction of evil in the demise of the serpent (Genesis 3:15), and he demonstrates his desire to continue involvement with his now sinful human creatures by providing them with garments to cover their now shameful nakedness.

LOOKING AHEAD

Adam and Eve's rebellion against God mars the harmony that existed between them and God with horrible consequences for their own relationship and their connection with the rest of creation. Indeed, people are no longer individually whole, experiencing self-alienation and death. Paul makes clear what is implicit in Genesis 3; that the story of Adam and Eve is about not only them as individuals but also all of humanity. After their rebellion, sin and death entered the world. Adam and Eve did what we would all do if we were in their place; and indeed, we all do sin. The stories that follow in Genesis 4–11 (Cain and Abel; the flood; the tower of Babel) all illustrate the pervasive character of human sin as well as God's judgment. These stories also speak of God's grace; he continues to be involved with them. He desires to restore a harmonious relationship with them.

This harmonious relationship and all that flows from it is bound up in the word *blessing*. When God created Adam and Eve, he blessed them (Genesis 1:28), but that blessing was shattered with their sin and the continued sin of humanity. God was not done with them, though. After considerable time, he chooses Abraham as the means through which he determines to bring blessing back to all humanity. It is to his story that we turn next.

Going Deeper

Longman, Tremper, III. *How to Read Genesis*. Downers Grove, IL: InterVarsity Press, 2005.

Walton, John H. *Genesis*. NIV Application Commentary. Grand Rapids: Zondervan, 2001.

3 / Abraham

Looking Ahead

MEMORY VERSE: Genesis 12:1-3
BIBLE STUDY: Genesis 12:1-3; 15; 17; 21:1-7; 22
READING: The Father of the Faith

 Bible Study Guide

After reading Genesis 12:1-3; 15; 17; 21:1-7; 22, spend some time reflecting on these passages with the following questions in mind before looking at the Reading. (For maximum benefit read Genesis 12:1–25:11.)

1. What does God promise to do for Abraham in Genesis 12:2-3?

2. What does God tell Abraham to do in order to receive the promises (Genesis 12:1)?

3. What does the promise that Abraham will become a "great nation" imply; that is, what has to happen for this promise to be realized?

4. According to Genesis 15:2-3 why does Abraham doubt God's ability or willingness to follow through on his promises?

5. How does God reassure Abraham (Genesis 15:4-5) and how does Abraham respond (Genesis 15:6)?

6. Notice that God shifts focus from Abraham having a son to the land in Genesis 15:7-8.

7. Visualize the ritual described in Genesis 15:9-21. Reflect on the significance of God's actions here.

8. In Genesis 16, Abraham took on a secondary wife named Hagar, who gave birth to a son Ishmael. Why do you think God didn't accept Ishmael as the promised heir to Abraham (Genesis 17:19-22)?

9. What is the significance of circumcision (Genesis 17:9-14)?

10. Why did God change Abram's name to Abraham and Sarai's name to Sarah (Genesis 17:5, 15)?

11. Why do you think God waited until Abraham and Sarah were so old to follow through on his promise that they would have a son (Genesis 21:1-7)?

12. What does Genesis 22 reveal about Abraham's faith?

⊙ Reading: The Father of the Faith

Genesis 12:1-3 is one of the most important passages in the entire Bible. Here God tells Abraham (at first called Abram) to leave his country, people and father's household and go to the "the land I will show you." Though there is some debate over whether his country is Ur in Mesopotamia or Haran, where they first went, there is no doubt about where God wants him to go. Canaan is the land of promise. While Ur and to a lesser extent Haran were more comfortable places to live, and Canaan something of a regional backwater, God had a great plan in mind. Abraham was to be the father of a new people through whom God intended to bring blessing to "all peoples on earth."

From our previous studies, we observed how God created humanity in a blessed condition, but they forfeited that blessing in their rebellion against him. God now purposes a way to restore that blessing through Abraham. Let's explore the promises that God makes to Abraham.

First, God promises to make Abraham a "great nation." What does it take to be a great nation? In the first place, land. The land to which God sends Abraham is not immediately his possession; he is a sojourner in it. But the promise indicates that his descendants will one day live in the land as permanent residents. In the second place, the promise requires many descendants. Later, when this aspect of the promise is reaffirmed, God will say that Abraham's descendants will be as many as the stars in heaven (Genesis 15:5 and elsewhere).

The other major element of God's promises to Abraham is blessing. In earlier studies I have described blessing as involving a harmonious relationship with God, with fellow humans and with creation. Adam and Eve in the Garden of Eden before their rebellion provides a picture of what a blessed life looks like. Importantly, God not only promises to bless Abraham and his descendants, but also all the nations of the earth. God is not choosing Abraham to the neglect of all his other human creatures; he is choosing Abraham to reach them all in order to restore relationship with them.

These are the promises that God makes to Abraham. While all aspects of the promises play a role in the Abraham story, the promise of descendants occupies a special place. Indeed, the promise of many descendants triggers a crisis of faith for Abraham because to have many future descendants, Abraham needs to have at least one child, and for reasons God does not explain, that first son does not come immediately or even in the following long years. Indeed, the account of Abraham's life is a story of his response to obstacles that threaten the fulfillment of the promises. Does Abraham respond with faith or fear?

Abraham responds to God's call by taking his wife and his nephew Lot to the Promised Land. At this point, Abraham is already seventy-five years old. He does not settle at one spot, but immediately moves from place to place. In the first few verses of his story, he lived first in Shechem in north central Palestine; then for a period of time he moved south, settling just east of Bethel, and finally much further south to the Negev (Genesis 12:4-9). Typically, the narrative mentions that he built an altar wherever he settled. One gets the feeling that though he is a wanderer in the land, he is marking it with altars to show that the land is God's.

While offspring will become the central focus of the narrative, the first two threats to the promise concern the land. Soon after Abraham arrives in the Promised Land, it is affected by a severe famine (Genesis 12:10-20). Abraham must move to Egypt. We can imagine the thoughts that must have run through his mind. God promised him this land, but it cannot sustain him. How does Abraham respond, with faith or fear? The answer is soon obvious as he turns to his wife and tells her to lie about her relationship with him. She tells the Egyptians she is Abraham's sister and not his wife, for fear that people will kill him to get at his wife. He does not trust God to take care of him. Nonetheless, God takes care of Abraham and Sarah, and protects them from harm, even enriching them. In a description that anticipates the later story of the exodus, Abraham goes down to Egypt because of a famine. God brings plague on Pharaoh and his court, and they return to Canaan enriched by the Egyptians.

In Genesis 13 we read of an episode of Abraham's life where he demonstrates trust rather than fear. Granted it is a different dilemma he faces. God has so enriched him that he and his nephew can no longer live in close proximity. They must divide the land. Now Abraham could have insisted that God gave him, and not Lot, the promise of the land, and he could have chosen the best part for himself. But he does not manipulate the fulfillment of the promise by grasping for the land. Instead, he rather magnanimously allows Lot to choose whatever part Lot wants. Lot chooses that lush land around the exciting cities of Sodom and Gomorrah.

The next part of the Abraham story that demonstrates his wavering faith in the fulfillment of the promises is Genesis 15. Some time has passed, and the chapter opens with God reassuring Abraham of his comforting presence (v. 1). But Abraham responds with doubt. He expresses his confusion over the fact that he and Sarah remain childless in spite of the divine promise. He then states that his servant Eliezer of Damascus will be his heir.

To understand Abraham's reasoning, it is important to know ancient customs of inheritance. Writings discovered by archaeologists that come from around the time and original homeland of Abraham (Haran) explain that childless couples would enter into a relationship with their household servant who would take care of them in their old age, and then inherit their property when they died. In other words, Abraham's statement to God was a way of telling him that he did not trust him to provide an heir any longer, so he would manufacture his own heir using the customs of the day.

God, though, repeats the promise that Abraham and Sarah will have their own child, and that ultimately their descendants will be many. Abraham's immediate response was one of trust, and, in a statement that will have great importance in New Testament theology, the narrator explains that "God credited it to him as righteousness" (v. 6; see "Anticipating the New Testament").

Then God instructs Abraham to take certain animals and cut them in half. After he lays the bloody body parts in two rows, we hear that "a smoking firepot with a blazing torch appeared and passed between the pieces" (v. 17). Then the narrator announces that God made a covenant with Abraham in which he reaffirmed the promise of land.

It is not surprising that modern readers are left bewildered at this point because, again, ancient Near Eastern custom stands behind God's actions. Ancient writings from the time period reveal that this ritual was a way for people to seal an important agreement. The thought behind it was that the two people who made the agreement would walk between the divided parts signifying that if they broke the agreement that they would be cut in half like the animals they walked through. Here, God is represented, as often through the early parts of the Bible, by fire and smoke, and it is only God who goes through the parts. In other words, God alone is committing to

Abraham that he will follow through on his solemn promises.

This agreement, by the way, is called a covenant. A covenant is a particular kind of agreement that is based on an ancient treaty. God the king has entered into a relationship with his subject Abraham. The actions in Genesis 15 are not so much a new relationship between God and Abraham, but a renewal of the promises made in Genesis 12:1-3.

The same may be said for Genesis 17. God again appears to Abraham and reassures him of his covenantal commitments. At the end of Genesis 15, we are left with the impression that Abraham had been properly reassured, but then in Genesis 16 we learn that he once again uses ancient customs to try to manipulate the production of an heir. This time he fathers a child with a concubine, or secondary wife, the Egyptian Hagar. In the ancient Near Eastern world, concubines were often used as a means of having children when one's wife was barren.

God's appearance to Abraham, though, was for the purpose of telling him once again that it would be with Sarah that God would give Abraham a legitimate heir. Thus, when the ninety-nine-year-old Abraham tries to convince God to accept Ishmael as his heir, God refuses, affirming yet again that the true heir would be born to him and Sarah. On the other hand, in keeping with God's original promise that he would bless the nations through Abraham, God makes it clear that he will also bless Ishmael and his descendants (Genesis 17:20), though the covenantal promises will pass down through Abraham's future son.

In the process of interaction with Abraham, God announces a change of name. Up to this point in the narrative, Abram, translated "exalted father," has been the name of the patriarch. God announces from henceforth he will be called Abraham, the "father of many," in keeping with the promise that states he will be the father of many descendants. Sarah also experiences a name change, but of a subtle kind. Sarai, "princess," will be called Sarah, "princess." The difference seems to be that the former means princess in an east Semitic dialect (associated with Ur of the Chaldeans from which they came), and Sarah is the west Semitic form (associated with the west Semitic region connected to the Promised Land).

Of course, the other notable feature of the second covenant renewal account in Genesis 17 is the establishment of circumcision, a ritual of great consequence during the Old Testament and into the Judaic period. Circumcision is called the sign of the covenant, which indicates that it is like a brand. Every time someone was circumcised, the brand of the Abrahamic covenant was presented, which made children of Abraham remember their duty to uphold their loyalty to Yahweh. A male child was to be circumcised on the eighth day (v. 12), signifying that it was a ritual that indicated that the child was initiated into the covenant community.

Circumcision makes sense in the present context where the focus of attention is on the birth of an heir. After all, the ritual

involves the removal of the foreskin of the male reproductive organ. I commented earlier that when God went through the divided parts in the form of a flaming torch in a smoking firepot he was taking a self-curse, in essence saying that if he did not follow through on his promises that he would become like those animals. Circumcision too is a self-curse, but this time performed on the human partner. The idea is that if a person breaks covenant with God, they would themselves be cut off from the covenant community, if not life itself.

Thus, at the end of chapter 17, God has yet again reassured the doubting Abraham of his commitment to fulfill the promises. Abraham's journey of faith has been up and down, alternating between trust and fear throughout his entire life. Indeed, just on the eve of the birth of the promised son, Abraham repeats his old strategy of lying about the status of his wife by telling her to say that she is his sister as he moves into foreign territory, this time the region of the Philistines (Genesis 20). As a matter of fact, when confronted, this time Abraham confesses that he has asked her to cover up for him "everywhere we go" (v. 13).

In spite of Abraham's struggles, God has protected him and stayed involved with him. Now, finally in his and Sarah's extreme old age, the promised child is born. Abraham was a hundred years old and Sarah was also ancient when Isaac was born. His name is connected with the Hebrew word for laughter, as Sarah says, "Everyone who hears about this will laugh with me" (Genesis 21:6).

Why would God wait so long to fulfill his promise? He could have done so immediately or at any point in Abraham's life. Was he simply torturing Abraham? Was he putting him through some kind of hideous test? No, the reason why God waited so long was to demonstrate that this child was indeed a gift from God. Only God could have provided the couple with a child at this point in their lives.

So the Abraham and Sarah story at last reaches its happy conclusion. The child is born, and the promises given in Genesis 12:1-3 can be passed down to the next generation and beyond.

However, as we read on we see the story of Abraham's life journey is not over. He is still to confront his most challenging moment yet when God tells him "Take your son, your only son, whom you love—Isaac—and go to the region of Moriah. Sacrifice him there as a burnt offering on a mountain I will show you" (Genesis 22:2).

How will Abraham respond? Some significant time has passed, as indicated by the fact that Isaac has grown up to the point that he can carry the firewood (v. 6). So perhaps now Abraham is over 110 years old. What hope would they have to have yet another child?

The narrative does not tell us what went through Abraham's mind. He might have been horrified at first, angry, frightened beyond imagination. But we only hear of his actions as he gets up the next day and gets supplies and Isaac and heads to the designated place to offer Isaac as a sacrifice to God. The main message of the narrative is that Abraham has come to a point at the end of his life when he utterly and completely trusts God.

His willingness to follow through on the divine command does not mean that he did not hold hope that God would stay his hand. We are to see glimmers of this hope in Abraham's statement to his servants, "Stay here with the donkey while I and the boy go over there. We will worship and then we will come back to you" (v. 5), as well as his response to Isaac's question concerning what they would sacrifice, "God himself will provide the lamb for the burnt offering" (v. 8).

Thus, though he "reached out his hand and took the knife to slay his son" (v. 10), imagine his joy when he was told not to follow through with the act. God did indeed provide a substitute, a ram caught in the thicket, and the heir does live and carry on the promises. Abraham has matured into a man of complete and utter faith.

Reading Study Guide

1. What are the promises that God makes to Abraham?

Why do you think he made Abraham leave his homeland and his family in order to receive these promises?

2. We have observed that the book of Genesis wants us to follow Abraham's life as a picture of the journey of his faith. Summarize in your own words this journey.

Does Abraham's life throw any light on your own faith journey?

3. We have seen how circumcision is a sign of the Abrahamic covenant. It indicated that a child was brought into the covenant community. Among Christians today baptism is a ritual of initiation into the covenant. What are the similarities and differences between these two rituals?

4. While the focus of the text is on Abraham (the patriarch), Sarah (the matriarch) is of course central to the story. How would you describe her role and her character as it is given in the book of Genesis?

5. God tells Abraham to take his son Isaac to Mount Moriah in order to sacrifice him there. The only other place Moriah is mentioned in the Bible is 2 Chronicles 3:1. Read this passage and discuss the significance of the connection between these two texts.

6. What is your emotional reaction to God's request to Abraham to offer his son Isaac as a sacrifice?

7. Can you see any parallel between God's command for Abraham to offer Isaac as a sacrifice and the cross of Jesus?

Anticipating the New Testament

Abraham was the father of the faith of the people of Israel. He received the covenantal promises of land, descendants and blessings. He occupied a critical place in the history of redemption that carries over into the New Testament. The New Testament often refers to him in order to teach important truths about Christian teaching and life.

Paul, in particular, cites Abraham as his prime example of the fact that we have a relationship with God through faith, not by our works. In Romans 4, he points out that Abraham "believed God, and it was credited to him as righteousness" (Romans 4:3, citing Genesis 15:6). It was not until later (Genesis 17) that Abraham was circumcised. God's grace, not our works, leads to a relationship with God through Christ.

The author of Hebrews gives Abraham an important place in his portrait gallery of those who demonstrate faith as "confidence in what we hope for and assurance about what we do not see" (Hebrews 11:1). Though, as we observed in our study of Genesis, Abraham was up and down in his faith, it is the latter that triumphs in his life, and thus he becomes a role model for all of us.

Finally, returning to Paul, we see that, while Isaac and the Israelites were a fulfillment of God's promise that Abraham would have descendants, Jesus is the ultimate fulfillment of this promise (Galatians 3:16). Further, if we are in a relationship with Jesus, then we too "are Abraham's seed, and heirs according to the promise" (Galatians 3:29). For further study, read Hebrews 11:1-12, 17-19; Romans 4; Galatians 3:15-29.

1. What does Abraham's life teach us about the relationship between faith and works?

2. How does Christ relate to the Abraham promise of descendants (see in particular Galatians 3:17)?

The Ancient Story and Our Story

Abraham is truly called the "father of the faith." God chose him out of all humanity to father a people (the Hebrews) whom God would bless and through whom God would bless "all the families on earth." The rest of the Old Testament and the New Testament tells the story of God bringing reconciliation between himself and his people. The New Testament will make it clear (see the following questions on Galatians 3:15-22) that Abraham is the father of the Christian faith as well.

Abraham's life also models the life of faith to us today, as will be further developed in relationship to Hebrews 11. We have already observed how the biblical account of Abraham follows his reactions to threats and obstacles to the fulfillment of the divine promises (Genesis 12:1-3). Sometimes he responds with fear and tries to manipulate the fulfillment of the promises, but other times he responds with faith. In spite of the ups and downs of Abraham's faith, God remains true to his promises. Christians today find themselves in a similar faith journey as Abraham. We too have a relationship with God who has given us promises, but sometimes, maybe even often, life does not seem to reflect God's love and care. We suffer pain and loss, as do those we love. Life is often difficult. How do we react? Do we react with faith? Do we react with fear? The story of Abraham encourages us to respond with faith as we remember that our God is a God who keeps his promises even if at times circumstances suggest otherwise.

Looking Ahead

Abraham received the promises of the covenant. While he eventually had a son, the full realization of the promises that his descendants would be a great nation and would be blessed and bring blessing to all the nations would be in the future. In the meantime what would happen to his immediate descendants? With that we turn our attention to the stories of Isaac and Jacob.

Going Deeper

Longman, Tremper, III. *How to Read Genesis*. Downers Grove, IL: InterVarsity Press, 2005.

Walton, John H. *Genesis*. NIV Application Commentary. Grand Rapids: Zondervan, 2001.

4 / Isaac and Jacob

LOOKING AHEAD

MEMORY VERSE: 1 Corinthians 1:27-29
BIBLE STUDY: Genesis 25:19-34; 26:34–27:46; 28:10-22; 29:14–30:24; 32:22-32; 35:1-14
READING: The Promise Continues

 ## Bible Study Guide

After reading Genesis 25:19-34; 26:34–27:46; 28:10-22; 29:14–30:24; 32:22-32; 35:1-14, spend some time reflecting on these passages with the following questions in mind before looking at the Reading. (For maximum benefit read Genesis 25:12–36:43.)

1. What does the opening story (Genesis 25:19-34) about Jacob and Esau tell the reader about their character and their relationship?

2. What do we learn about the attitudes of Rebekah, Jacob and Esau in the story in Genesis 26:34–27:46?

   What is the future significance of Jacob's theft of the blessing?

3. Why does Jacob have to go to Haran?

4. What does God tell Jacob when he encounters him at Bethel, and what commitment does Jacob make to God (Genesis 28:1-22)?

5. How has Jacob used deception in the story to get his way?

How does Laban use deception against Jacob (Genesis 29:13–30:24)?

6. How would you characterize the dynamics of Jacob's family after he marries both Leah and Rachel?

7. Use the following questions to explain in your own words the wrestling match between Jacob and "the man" in Genesis 32:22-32: Who is "the man"? Why are they fighting? What is the outcome? Why does the man change Jacob's name to Israel?

8. What does Jacob do when he returns to Bethel (Genesis 35:1-15)? What is the significance of his actions?

Reading: The Promise Continues

The reading picks up some highlights of the accounts of Isaac's and Jacob's lives, and in this essay I will place these episodes in the larger whole. While particularly Isaac but also Jacob do not play as large a role in the book of Genesis as Abraham, all three of them, Abraham, Isaac and Jacob, are considered the patriarchs of the faith in later Old Testament times. The thread that holds the stories of Abraham, Isaac and Jacob together is the passing down and continuity of the covenant promises that God gives Abraham in Genesis 12:1-3. Of course, the stories of Isaac and his son overlap with each other, and one of the major concerns of the narrative is the question why Jacob rather than Esau, just as earlier the question was why Isaac rather than Ishmael? In terms of the former question, we will see, in the language of the memory verse, that God chose the "foolish" to shame the "wise" (1 Corinthians 1:27-29).

As we saw in the previous study, the story of Abraham focused on the birth of an heir who would inherit the covenant promises (Genesis 21:12; 25:11; 26:4). That long-awaited son was Isaac, and by the time we read of Abraham's death (Genesis 25:1-11), we are already acquainted with his son. Indeed, Genesis 24 presents the touching story of Isaac's marriage to Rebekah. That said, it is interesting to note how little of the biblical story focuses in on Isaac. Up to now he has been Abraham's

son, and once we hear of his father's death, he becomes Jacob's father. In other words, the real attention of the biblical narrator is Jacob, not Isaac. Even so, Isaac is an important link between these two important and interesting characters, and he does pass down the promise from his father to his son. But the latter transition does not take place easily or simply.

Like Sarah, his mother, Isaac's wife Rebekah is barren. Though not waiting until her advanced old age, God opens her womb, demonstrating that these important children are God's gift. She gives birth to twins (Genesis 25:21-26). While the older is Esau, God makes it clear to Rebekah at the time of the babies' birth that the younger, Jacob, will be the dominant one. Esau means "hairy," while his second name Edom, means "red," pointing to his abundant body hair as well as to his red complexion. Jacob's name is connected to the fact that he grabbed his older twin's heel as he came out of the womb; thus his name means "he grasps the heel." In the light of his actions as an adult, the name might also be connected with the verb "deceives." Indeed, Jacob, as well as Esau's character, is revealed in the very next story set in the two boys' early adulthood. Jacob takes advantage of Esau's obsession with the sensuous and immediate gratification when Esau sells his birthright for some bread and lentil soup (Genesis 25:27-34). While it is unclear whether this purchase would have any legal standing, it does set up the story about Jacob's theft of Esau's blessing. The burning question is through which of these two children will the covenant promises flow into the next generation. The cultural expectation would be that Esau, the older, would dominate, but the divine oracle at birth (Genesis 25:23) has pointed to the younger Jacob.

Even so, when it came time for the elderly and nearly blind Isaac to confer his blessing upon the chosen child, he called for Esau. Rebekah overheard her husband tell Esau to go to the field, since he was an outdoorsman, to hunt game to prepare a tasty dish for his father to eat. She then quickly instructs Jacob on how to deceive his father into giving him the blessing instead. Before too quickly judging Rebekah, we should remember that she heard God's intention for Jacob at the time of his birth. Thus, to bless Esau would seem to undermine the divine intention. That said, what she advises Jacob does seem a desperate deception in keeping with his name.

She fixed the tasty dish while Jacob was fitted with a hairy chest piece, anticipating that the blind Isaac would do a touch test to make sure that the son he was blessing was Esau. Jacob and Rebekah successfully pull off their ruse, so Isaac blesses the younger son. When Esau returns from the field, he is filled with anger and thoughts of revenge toward his younger brother, so his mother talks Isaac into letting him go to their near relatives' dwelling in Paddan Aram, where he can find a wife. Rebekah has urged him to leave to escape his broth-

er's anger, and she tells Isaac that it is best for Jacob to leave to avoid marrying a Canaanite as his brother Esau has done. Significantly, Isaac blesses Jacob again, conferring on him the covenant promises, as he departs (Genesis 28:3-4).

Jacob's first personal encounter with God takes place on his way to Paddan Aram. Before he leaves the boundaries of the Promised Land, God appears to Jacob while he is sleeping. In his dream he saw a stairway with its top in heaven and angels going up and down on it. Above the stairway, God spoke to Jacob affirming Isaac's words that it will be Jacob through whom the promises will pass:

> I am the LORD, the God of your father Abraham and the God of Isaac. I will give you and your descendants the land on which you are lying. Your descendants will be like the dust of the earth, and you will spread out to the west and to the east, to the north and to the south. All peoples on earth will be blessed through you and your offspring. I am with you and will watch over you wherever you go, and I will bring you back to this land. I will not leave you until I have done what I promised you. (Genesis 28:13-15; compare Genesis 12:1-3)

In response, Jacob named this holy spot Bethel, or "House of God," and promised that if God brought him back to the land safely that he would worship the Lord as his God.

Jacob then finished his journey to Paddan Aram, and as soon as he arrived there, he met Rachel, the daughter of his uncle Laban, at a well. Jacob fell deeply in love with Rachel and committed to working for seven years for his uncle in order to receive her as his wife. However, after the seven years, Jacob, who had deceived his father, is himself deceived by his uncle. In the dark on the wedding night, Laban had substituted Rachel's older sister Leah into his bed. Jacob had no love for Leah, who is described as having "weak eyes" (Genesis 29:17), an idiom that indicates she was unattractive, though the precise meaning is unclear. Laban appeals to the custom of his area that the older sister must marry first and then agrees to give Jacob Rachel immediately on condition of seven more years of labor.

The rivalry between the two sisters initiates a "baby war." This conflict, resulting ultimately in the birth of twelve sons, has great impact on the future people of God, as we will see. Eleven of them were born in quick succession.

God had pity on the unloved Leah and allowed her to have babies, while Rachel's womb remained closed. Leah has four sons to start: Reuben, Simeon, Levi and Judah. In desperation Rachel gave Jacob a concubine, who would have babies on her behalf. Bilhah gave birth to Dan and Naphtali. Leah, in her turn, gave Jacob a second concubine, Zilpah. Zilpah gave birth to Gad and Asher. Rachel agreed to allow Leah to sleep with Jacob in exchange for some mandrakes, which she probably thought would help her conceive. Leah then had a fifth child, namely Issachar, and even a sixth, named Zebulun. At long last, God allowed Rachel to have her first child and that child was Joseph. As we will see in study 5, Joseph would become the favorite child of Jacob, causing even further family strife.

Soon Jacob wants to leave Paddan Aram and return home (see Genesis 30:25-26). Of course, Laban does not want him to go since he realizes that his own wealth and prosperity are the result of Jacob's presence with him. He now agrees to pay Jacob for his labor in something other than wives to induce him to stay. Jacob takes this as an opportunity to deceive his uncle.

Jacob requests that he be paid in sheep and goats. He suggests that he get all the speckled and spotted sheep, every dark-colored lamb and every spotted or speckled goat. That way, he claims, Laban will be certain that no deception is involved since it will be obvious which belong to Jacob and which belong to Laban. However, Jacob has a trick up his sleeve. He placed "fresh-cut branches from poplar, almond and plane trees and made white stripes on them by peeling the bark and exposing the inner wood of the branches" (Genesis 30:37). When the animals mated in front of these branches, lo and behold they came out spotted, speckled or dark-colored! The bottom line was that Jacob's flock flourished while Laban's diminished. One might ask what was behind Jacob's strategy. How did it work? From a modern scientific perspective it shouldn't have worked. It may have been an ancient belief, but there really was nothing in the branches that would have affected the animals' offspring. Thus, we conclude that God made it all work out, not Jacob's ploy.

Needless to say, not only Laban but his sons were dismayed at these developments, and they turned angry toward Jacob, only fueling his desire to leave and return home to the Promised Land. Even more importantly, God himself told him that the time had come to return (Genesis 31:3). Leah and Rachel agreed, having no love for their father. So Jacob again deceived Laban by stealing away without informing him.

When Laban heard about Jacob and his family's departure, he took off in hot pursuit and overtook Jacob before he reentered the Promised Land. Laban was ready for vengeance, but was restrained by God himself who told him not to harm Jacob (v. 24). Laban was particularly upset by the theft of his household idols. As readers, we have been informed that Rachel indeed did steal the idols, though she is the only one of her family who knew about it (v. 19). We are not told why she stole them. Later custom that might apply to this time period stated that the possessor of the idols would inherit the estate, but it is more likely that she simply wanted to take something of value from her father out of spite toward him. It is also possible that Rachel herself was still worshiping idols (see Genesis 35:2-3). Whatever the reason, Jacob vehemently denied the charge, not knowing about Rachel's act. Rachel deceives her father by hiding the idols in her saddle on

which she sat, asking not to move because she was having her period. A later Israelite reader would understand that this demeaned those idols, since a woman having her period was considered ritually unclean (Leviticus 15:19). After unsuccessfully searching for the idols, Laban then enters into a treaty relationship with Jacob, having implications for later Israelite-Aramean relationships.

Having resolved the conflict with Laban in Paddan Aram, Jacob now returns to the Promised Land to face his brother, Esau, who is bearing down on him from the other direction. Rebekah had urged Jacob to flee his homeland to Paddan Aram in the first place because she had heard of Esau's intention to kill Jacob for stealing the blessing from his father (Genesis 27:41-45).

Jacob had alerted Esau about his return to the land. Perhaps he was encouraged to do so after he encountered angels from God as he moved on from his meeting with Laban. He named the place Mahanaim, which means "two camps," referring to his as well as to the angels' (Genesis 32:1-2).

Esau's response to Jacob's message was deeply unsettling. Jacob's messengers informed him that Esau was moving toward him with four hundred men. Thinking that Esau was coming with hostile intent, Jacob took measures designed to minimize the damage. He divided his family, servants and property into two parts, so if one was attacked the other might escape.

He also turned to God in prayer to ask

for his protection, reminding him that it was he who told him to return to the Promised Land. He also sent gifts of herds and flocks in front of him hoping that these would also satisfy his brother.

Having devised and executed his strategy of appeasement, Jacob spent the night alone before the encounter with his brother. That night brought an unexpected and enigmatic conflict with "a man" who wrestled with him until dawn (Genesis 32:22-32). Most mysterious is the identity of the man. In the end, the text is clear that God has taken the form of a man who wrestles Jacob. The man says, for instance, "you have struggled with God and with humans and have overcome" (v. 28). The man also blesses Jacob, which demonstrates that he is the superior person (v. 29). On the other hand, the man could not overpower Jacob, which of course, God could clearly do. Perhaps we are to think that God intentionally limited his power to teach Jacob a lesson. Jacob certainly understood that he had fought God, because he names the place Peniel, the "face of God," and says, "I saw God face to face, and yet my life was spared" (v. 30).

The man, that is God himself, gives Jacob a new name, Israel. Israel is the father of twelve sons, who represent the tribes of the future nation. Israel means "God fights," appropriate not only for this story but for the future of Israel on whose behalf God will fight against their enemies.

After fighting God, Jacob/Israel now faces Esau. In a word, Jacob's prayers were answered as Esau ran up to him not to fight him but to embrace him, even refusing the gifts that Jacob had given him. God had blessed both Esau and Jacob, so Esau's animosity had died down. Even so, Jacob insisted on giving the gifts.

Esau wanted Jacob to come with him to his homeland in Seir, which is outside the Promised Land, but Jacob instead went near the Canaanite city of Shechem and settled there. God wants Jacob in the Promised Land, not in Seir, but the text is silent as to whether Jacob's actions constitute another act of deception on his part or whether the invitation was socially polite. What is clear is that Jacob and Esau are no longer in conflict, and when their father Isaac dies, both "his sons Esau and Jacob buried him" (Genesis 35:29).

Trouble comes to Jacob in Shechem (Genesis 34). His daughter Dinah goes into the Canaanite town with some Canaanite girlfriends and is raped by the son of the ruler of that city, enraging her full brothers, Levi and Simeon, who ultimately get vengeance for their sister by slaughtering the men of the city. This story has implications for the choice of the Levites as priests and is treated more fully in study 9, on "Priests, Holy Place and Sacrifice." For now, we should note that Jacob's actions demonstrate that he was getting much too cozy with the Canaanites, and God used the brothers to prevent Jacob from intermarrying with them or becoming too comfortable living in their midst.

Indeed, the final story of the Jacob narrative concerns his recommitment to the proper worship of the true God. When

Jacob had originally left the Promised Land to go to Paddan Aram, he made the following commitment after he had an experience of God's presence at the town of Bethel:

> If God will be with me and will watch over me on this journey I am taking and will give me food to eat and clothes to wear so that I return safely to my father's household, then the LORD will be my God and this stone that I have set up as a pillar will be God's house, and of all that you give me I will give you a tenth. (Genesis 28:20-22)

God had brought him home safely, but Jacob did not rush to fulfill this vow. Indeed, God had to come remind him of it (Genesis 35:1). Jacob did respond to God's call first of all by divesting his family of all their false gods and telling them to purify themselves. Jacob then went to Bethel where he built an altar to God, and God in his turn reaffirmed the covenant promises of descendants and land (Genesis 35:11-13; compare Genesis 12:1-3).

Finally, we read that Rachel had a twelfth and final child, Benjamin, but she died in childbirth. In the final section of Genesis, Jacob remains an important figure, but the plot now focuses on his sons, particularly Joseph.

Reading Study Guide

1. What makes Isaac and Jacob important figures in the book of Genesis and the rest of the Bible?

2. What is the significance of the fact that Rebekah, like Sarah, is barren?

3. What is the meaning of the name Esau and the meaning of the name Jacob?

How does the meaning of their names play into the message of their story?

4. What do Esau's actions demonstrate about how important the covenant promises are to him?

5. Esau has often been described as a "sensual" person. What would lead to that assessment?

Is there anything in the story that leads you to think he is spiritual rather than sensual?

6. Rebekah encourages and helps Jacob deceive Isaac. How do you evaluate her decisions and actions?

Is she doing the right thing? Why or why not?

7. Describe Jacob's first direct and personal encounter with God.

8. What does the "baby war" between Leah and Rachel tell us about polygamy?

9. Why does Laban's household prosper while Jacob lives there?

10. Deception plays a big role in the Jacob story. List all the times a character deceives another.

Sometimes good results come from deception. Does that make lying acceptable? Why or why not?

11. How did Jacob receive the new name Israel?

What is the significance of the new name?

➡ Anticipating the New Testament

Ishmael was the product of Abraham's manipulation of the social customs of the day. Not willing to wait for God's fulfillment of the promise of an heir, Abraham took a concubine and had a child Ishmael. Though Abraham wanted God to accept Ishmael as his heir, God refused, knowing that at the right time Abraham and Sarah would have a child, Isaac, and through this child the covenant promises would pass down to the following generations.

1. According to Galatians 4:21-31, what does it mean to be the child of the slave woman? Of the free woman?

If we look at it honestly, we have to see that Jacob is a scoundrel. He deceives and manipulates the people with whom he comes into contact. He shows favorites: he favors Rachel over Leah, and in the next study we will see him favor Joseph and Benjamin over his other sons. He has nothing to commend him to us or to God. Yet he is the one through whom the covenant promises pass from his father to the next generation. He is a prime example of how God chooses the foolish, the lowly and the weak to further his plans for the world (see 1 Corinthians 1:27-28).

God's choice of Jacob rather than Esau is surprising, not only because Jacob was a scoundrel but also because he was the second-born to Esau. According to the customs of the day, the firstborn inherited the lion's share of his parent's property. But here Jacob, the second-born, gets the inheritance that really matters. He will be the one through whom the covenant promises will flow to future generations. (For more on God's choices read Romans 9:6-29.)

2. Is it encouraging or discouraging to you that God uses the foolish, the lowly, the weak and the second-born?

The Ancient Story and Our Story

Our memory verse (1 Corinthians 1:27-29) expresses an important principle that remains relevant for modern readers and is illustrated by the Isaac and Jacob story. God chooses the foolish things to shame the wise. Jacob strikes a foolish figure in the book of Genesis. God chooses the weak things of the world to shame the strong. On the surface, Esau was the stronger, while Jacob was the weaker, younger brother. As we discussed, Isaac, Jacob's father, also comes across as weak and foolish. Modern readers should be encouraged by the example of these two men, because if we are honest, we should recognize our own folly and weakness. Why would God want or need to use us for his purposes? But he does. And when he does, we should continue to remember that we are weak, foolish people; otherwise we will be filled with pride. Why does God use the foolish and weak? Because, as God said to Paul concerning his weakness, "My grace is sufficient for you, for my power is made perfect in weakness" (2 Corinthians 12:9). Therefore, "no one may boast before him" (1 Corinthians 1:29), but "let the one who boasts boast in the Lord" (1 Corinthians 1:31, citing Jeremiah 9:24).

Looking Ahead

Though Isaac has not been an active character in the story for some chapters now, Genesis 35 ends with an account of his death, bringing the narrative to a temporary pause. As I mentioned earlier, Rachel also died giving birth to her final child Benjamin. Jacob is still alive and will play a role in the final major section of the book of Genesis. Even so, after a chapter of genealogies devoted to Esau's line (Genesis 36), the focus of attention shifts from Jacob to his twelve sons and one in particular, Joseph.

Going Deeper

Longman, Tremper, III. *How to Read Genesis*. Downers Grove, IL: InterVarsity Press, 2005.
Walton, John H. *Genesis*. NIV Application Commentary. Grand Rapids: Zondervan, 2001.

5 / Joseph

LOOKING AHEAD

MEMORY VERSE: Genesis 50:19-20
BIBLE STUDY: Genesis 37; 39; 45; 49:29–50:20
READING: The Promise Survives

 ## Bible Study Guide

After reading Genesis 37; 39; 45; 49:29–50:20, spend some time reflecting on these passages with the following questions in mind before looking at the Reading. (For maximum benefit read Genesis 37–50.)

1. Why do Joseph's brothers hate him so much?

   Does Joseph do anything to deserve this?

2. What is the significance of Joseph's dreams in chapter 37?

3. What roles do Reuben, the firstborn son, and Judah play when the brothers sell Joseph to the Ishmaelites who are heading to Egypt?

4. Why was Joseph so successful as a servant in the household of Potiphar?

5. Why do you think Potiphar's wife framed Joseph?

6. Why do you think Joseph hid his identity from his brothers when they first arrived in Egypt?

7. Why were the brothers afraid of Joseph after Jacob died?

8. Where did Joseph find the strength to forgive his brothers for the horrible things that they did to him?

👓 Reading: The Promise Survives

The first thought that comes into many people's minds today when they think of Joseph is his multicolored robe, made famous by a musical by Andrew Lloyd Webber. Hebrew scholars today doubt that that is the proper understanding of the rare Hebrew word that was traditionally so translated, but no matter what exactly this outer garment looked like (long-sleeved?), it was clearly a sign of Jacob's favoritism for the son born to his beloved Rachel. Joseph was indeed favored, and his brothers were jealous to the point of hatred. Joseph did little to soften their hatred, so when he had two dreams that announced his future preeminence over his brothers, he did not hold back a public announcement. Here we see the origins, though not the excuse, of the horrible deed that the brothers will commit against their brother.

And it is just the first of many horrible things that will happen to Joseph, as we will see. But before we review Joseph's life as narrated in Genesis 37–50, we need to race forward to the end. Here we will learn the main theme of this last portion of Genesis from the mouth of Joseph himself.

After the death of their father, Jacob, the brothers are deeply frightened. They reason that Joseph has withheld his vengeance these many years on account of their father. So they approach Joseph as a group, beg his forgiveness and offer themselves as his slaves. In response, Joseph tells them: "Don't be afraid. Am I in the place of God? You intended to harm me, but God intended it for good to accomplish what is now being done, the saving of many lives" (Genesis 50:19-20). Toward the end of his life Joseph could look back on all the horrible things that happened to him and say that it was the result of God's providence. God used these very actions in order to bring about salvation. It is in the light of this perspective that we will look at the Joseph narrative.

We return now to the beginning of the story. We have seen that the brothers were deeply angered by their father's favoritism toward Joseph. They soon had an opportunity to act on their jealous hatred of Joseph when they were shepherding their father's flocks far away from their home in the vicinity of the city of Shechem. Joseph did not go with them, but he was sent by his father to check on them. He caught up with them in Dothan. As they saw him coming from a distance, they began to plot what to do with him. The brothers immediately think of killing him, throwing him into a nearby cistern and then telling their father that he had been killed by a wild animal. Reuben the oldest intervened to keep them from killing him but agreed to throw him into the cistern. Reuben was the oldest son of Jacob and the one who was responsible for the others. Secretly he planned to come back and free Joseph, but Judah, the fourth born, convinced the brothers, apparently in the absence of

Reuben, to sell Joseph to a caravan of traders who were heading down to Egypt, thus foiling the older brother's plan of rescue. We will keep our eye on Reuben and Judah in this story because a secondary theme of the story that centers on Joseph concerns the relationship between these two as well as their development as individuals.

Indeed, the fact that Judah is an important figure in the story explains why a whole chapter (Genesis 38) tells a story about him apart from his brothers, and the story does not flatter Judah. After all, he marries a Canaanite girl who gives birth to a number of boys. The oldest, Er, marries a woman named Tamar. However, since Er was evil, God had him put to death. According to ancient custom, the childless Tamar was then married to Er's brother Onan. But Onan did not follow through on his obligation to Tamar and did not impregnate her. Thus God had him put to death as well. Judah then refused to let another one of his sons marry Tamar, leaving her without a husband and without a son, a precarious position for a woman in that society. Tamar took matters into her own hands. She dressed like a prostitute and fooled Judah into sleeping with her. Judah had left his seal, its cord and his staff as assurance that he would pay what he thought was a prostitute but who in reality was his daughter-in-law. Later, when it was announced that Tamar was pregnant, Judah wanted her executed—until she presented him with the objects that identified him as the father. In response, Judah announced, "She is more righteous than I." He had not given her his next son Selah, and he slept with a prostitute who turned out to be his daughter-in-law. So Judah both instigated Joseph's sale to the Ishmaelites, and he acted inappropriately toward his daughter-in-law. At the beginning of the Joseph narrative, Judah's character is quite dubious.

Genesis 39 shifts its attention back to Joseph. He has been sold by the Ishmaelites to Potiphar, a high Egyptian official. Potiphar's title literally translates as "chief butcher," indicating some kind of military function. Joseph, though, captures his respect and perhaps even his affection, because under Joseph's guidance the household of Potiphar achieved great success. But the reasons go far beyond the fact that Joseph was a dutiful and capable servant. The passage goes to great lengths to say that "the LORD was with Joseph" (vv. 2-3), and for this reason God blessed Joseph's efforts (v. 5). With these words the narrator is reminding us that Joseph is a son of the covenant promises and a recipient of the blessings of God.

However, Potiphar's wife had evil intentions toward Joseph. She found him attractive and attempted to seduce him. Joseph responded as he should by refusing her. Indeed, the book of Proverbs (chapters 5–7) warns the godly, wise man not to sleep with the foreign, strange woman. But the story takes a turn for the worse when she frames him for attempted rape and Joseph gets sent off to prison.

Potiphar's wife, like Joseph's brothers, acted with evil intentions (they meant it for evil), but in retrospect Joseph (and the reader) can see that God is moving with purpose here (God meant it for good). In prison Joseph comes into contact with two high Egyptian officials who had displeased Pharaoh. Again, Joseph shows himself to be an interpreter of dreams, when he tells the chief cupbearer that his dream indicated that he would be freed from prison, but that the chief baker's dream revealed that he would lose his head. As these events unfold, Joseph tells the departing chief cupbearer to remember to help him when he is on the outside.

But yet again Joseph is disappointed in his expectations when the chief cupbearer forgets all about him, until Pharaoh himself has two dreams that he cannot interpret. At that point the cupbearer remembers Joseph, who successfully interprets the king's dreams. The dreams both indicated that a period of abundance would be followed by a period of severe famine. The warning allows Pharaoh to prepare for the famine, and he chooses Joseph to head up this effort, appointing him to be "in charge of the whole land of Egypt" (Genesis 41:41). Joseph then successfully prepares for the famine and is in position to dole out the stored grain to the Egyptians and others. At this point the story turns back to the family in Canaan.

In Genesis 42 we learn that the famine has also hit Canaan hard. When Jacob hears that there is grain in Egypt, he sends his sons to buy some so the family can survive. We also learn that Jacob is still up to his old games, because he keeps his new favorite son, Benjamin, like Joseph a son of Rachel, safely back home with him.

When they arrive in Egypt, they are received by Joseph, who recognizes them, though they do not recognize him. After all, he has taken on Egyptian dress and appearance. He does not tell them who he is but rather accuses them of being spies. They plead with him that they are just ordinary people and in the process mention Benjamin, their younger brother. Joseph tells them that they must bring Benjamin to him in order to prove the truth of their claims, and he takes Simeon as a hostage. They return with grain. When they get back to Jacob and they open the grain, they see their payment also in the sacks. They are mystified and frightened. They tell Jacob they must take Benjamin down to Egypt, but he refuses to place his favorite son in jeopardy, even if it means forfeiting Simeon.

However, eventually the grain runs out and they must return to Egypt. Jacob is distraught, but Judah, not Reuben the firstborn as might be expected, steps forward and takes responsibility for Benjamin. Jacob yields to the inevitable and allows them to go.

Joseph receives them again and continues to hide his true identify from them. He gives them grain, but then sets them up by placing his diviner's cup in Benjamin's sack of grain. After they leave for Canaan, Joseph sends out one of his servants to stop them and accuse them of theft. They deny it, but agree that if the cup is found in any one of their sacks, then that person will be Joseph's prisoner. The servant discovers Joseph's cup in Benjamin's sack, and he is taken prisoner.

While the narrator does not come out and explicitly state Joseph's motives, it is clear that he is testing them to see whether they have changed their ways since they sold him to Egypt. He now has them in a comparable position. The fate of Jacob's new favorite son is in their hands. Will they abandon him, not caring whether he remains a prisoner? Do they not care about their father? Do they feel remorse about all the pain that they have made Joseph endure?

Judah steps forward to answer all these questions. In a lengthy and passionate speech (Genesis 44:18-34), Judah offers himself in place of Benjamin. He does not want to go back and see his father's pain at the loss of his favorite son.

Here we witness a remarkable transformation in the character of Judah from the beginning of the Joseph narrative to the end. We noted that at the beginning he was the one who engineered the selling of Joseph, thwarting Reuben's hidden plan to rescue Joseph and bring him home safely. Even worse was his treatment of his daughter-in-law Tamar. But his character has matured over the years since, and here he stands ready to sacrifice on behalf of his brothers.

The significance of his maturation is that the tribe of Judah in the future will be the most important of all the tribes from a leadership perspective. This role needs explanation since Judah is not the firstborn but rather the fourth-born son of Jacob/Israel. Even beginning with Genesis 49:8-10, we have anticipation that Judah will be the tribe from which Israel's future kings will come (see study 12).

In response to Judah's speech, Joseph reveals his identity to his brothers. They are understandably startled and terrified. The brother they had abused was now in a position of almost absolute power over them. But he assures them, anticipating his climactic words in Genesis 50:19-20, but assuring them that "God sent me ahead of you to preserve for you a remnant on earth and to save your lives by a great deliverance" (Genesis 45:7). He then instructs them to go back to Jacob and bring the whole family to Egypt. Jacob too is overwhelmed when he is reunited with Joseph. The Pharaoh allows the family to emigrate to Egypt and gives them land fitting for them as shepherds, the land of Goshen.

Now in retrospect, Joseph sees God's hand at work in his difficult life. Horrible things happened to him at the hands of people with evil intentions. His brothers sold him, Potiphar's wife framed him, the chief cupbearer forgot about him, but all these things happened for a good purpose. God did not do an end run around these evil acts, he actually used them to accomplish the rescue of his chosen people. God's providence does not excuse the actions of evil people, but it reminds those who read Joseph's story that good things can come out of horrible circumstances.

And here God's providence assured the survival of the chosen family. If they had died, then the covenantal promises would have come to an end unfulfilled. But God's promises do not go unfulfilled. Through his intervention behind the scenes and working in the most remarkable and surprising manner, God used even the actions of evil people to bring about his purposes.

The Joseph narrative serves yet another purpose in the Pentateuch. We always need to remember that the five books of the Pentateuch do not stand alone but are a part of the larger literary unity of the whole Torah, the first five books of the Bible. The Joseph narrative explains why and how God's people came to Egypt. When the book of Exodus opens many years later in Egypt, the book of Genesis has provided the background.

Indeed, the book of Genesis ends with some sense of closure but also the anticipation of a sequel. The closure comes from the report that Joseph died, thus bringing to a conclusion the period of time that occupied the interest of the final part of the book of Genesis (Genesis 50:26). The anticipation of the sequel comes from Joseph's final words to his brothers, "'I am about to die. But God will surely come to your aid and take you up out of this land to the land he promised on oath to Abraham, Isaac and Jacob.' And Joseph made the Israelites swear an oath and said, 'God will surely come to your aid, and then you must carry my bones up from this place'" (vv. 24-25). The book of Exodus will narrate the time when the Israelites will return to the promised land, taking with them the bones of Joseph.

Reading Study Guide

1. Is it fair to call Joseph a brat in his interaction with his brothers in Genesis 37? If so, does this absolve the brothers of guilt in their treatment of Joseph?

2. As you read through the Joseph narrative, do you see any growth in the character of Joseph?

   What about Judah?

3. What is the main theme of the Joseph narrative?

4. The main theme of the Joseph narrative is that God can use even evil deeds to bring about the rescue or salvation of people. Can you think of any other Old Testament examples where God uses the evil deeds of people for good purposes?

5. What is the significance of the fact that God was "with Joseph" as he served in the household of Potiphar?

6. How is Joseph a role model for our actions and character today?

7. Why didn't Joseph reveal his identity to his brothers when they came to Egypt for the first time?

   Do you think he was fair with them?

8. How does the Joseph narrative portray Jacob's character?

   Do you feel any sympathy for him? Why or why not?

9. Does the fact that God used Joseph's brothers' evil intentions for good exonerate them from guilt? Why or why not?

Anticipating the New Testament

In our study of the Joseph narrative, we saw that the main theme was "you intended to harm me, but God intended it for good to accomplish what is now being done, the saving of many lives" (Genesis 50:20). It wasn't simply that God accomplished his redemptive goal in spite of the evil actions of the brothers, Potiphar's wife and others; he actually used them.

Peter recognizes that God also used the sinful actions of wicked people in the most important redemptive act of all, the death and resurrection of Christ. He was put to death "with the help of wicked men," but God raised him from the dead, and his death and resurrection saves the many who put their faith in him (see Acts 2:22-24).

What God did in Joseph's life, he can also do in ours. In a well-known passage Paul tells the Roman church: "We know that in all things God works for the good of those who love him, who have been called according to his purpose" (Romans 8:28).

1. Is it encouraging or discouraging that God can use the wicked actions of others to bring about good things in our lives?

2. Does the fact that God can use evil actions for his good purpose mean that people should not be held responsible for their evil? Explain.

⬭ The Ancient Story and Our Story

As we studied earlier, the main theme of the Joseph story as expressed in Genesis 50:20 is "you intended to harm me, but God intended it for good to accomplish what is now being done, the saving of many lives." Joseph's story reminds us that even the bad things that happen to us can have positive, redemptive consequences. We learn that we are not simply cast about by chance fate, but we are in the hands of God. Such a perspective on life can give us the strength to endure even in the most difficult of times and helps us to put to practice James's instruction, "Consider it pure joy, my brothers and sisters, whenever you face trials of many kinds, because you know that the testing of your faith produces perseverance. Let perseverance finish its work so that you may be mature and complete, not lacking anything" (James 1:2-4).

While Joseph could look over his life and see clearly the good that God brought out of the horrible experiences of his life, most of us will go to the grave without an explanation. Our suffering appears meaningless. However, Christian hope extends beyond the grave. In other words, we need to develop an eschatological (future-oriented) hope. This life is not the end. Our perspective is now limited and finite. In the words of Paul, "now we see only a reflection as in a mirror," but in the age to come "we shall see face to face" (1 Corinthians 13:12).

Only from that future viewpoint will we make sense of our lives. But let me suggest that most if not all of us can look back on our lives and remember events that we thought were bad, but in the long run we came to see were actually for our good. Perhaps here we get glimpses of something that Joseph saw in a broader sense in his life and how we will all come to see in the age to come.

LOOKING AHEAD

We have now come to the end of the book of Genesis, the foundation to the rest of the Pentateuch and, indeed, to the whole Bible. As mentioned in the Reading, the ending of Genesis leaves us with a strong expectation of a sequel, and Exodus satisfies that expectation. When we turn to study 6, we find the descendants of Abraham, Isaac, Jacob and Joseph have become a large population, but they are enslaved to their former Egyptian hosts.

Going Deeper

Longman, Tremper, III. *How to Read Genesis*. Downers Grove, IL: InterVarsity Press, 2005.
Walton, John H. *Genesis*. NIV Application Commentary. Grand Rapids: Zondervan, 2001.

6 / Exodus

Looking Ahead

MEMORY VERSE: Exodus 15:1-4
BIBLE STUDY: Exodus 1; 3; 12; 13:17–15:22
READING: God Saves His People from Bondage

 ## Bible Study Guide

After reading Exodus 1; 3; 12; 13:17–15:22, spend some time reflecting on these passages with the following questions in mind before looking at the Reading. (For maximum benefit read Exodus 1–18.)

1. Read Exodus 1:7. Does the language used here remind you of anything in the book of Genesis?

2. Read Exodus 1:8-10. What is different among the Israelites since the end of the book of Genesis?

3. Read Exodus 1:15-22. The midwives lie to save the lives of male Hebrew babies. Does God approve of their lying?

4. Is there anything familiar about God appearing to Moses in the burning bush (Exodus 3)?

5. Why does Moses hesitate to accept God's call to return to Egypt?

Is he reasonable?

6. What is the significance of God revealing his name to Moses from the burning bush?

7. How is the style of writing in Exodus 12 different from the previous chapters?

8. Exodus 12 concerns the final plague, the death of the firstborn. What does verse 12 say about the purpose of these plagues?

9. According to Exodus 14:1-4, why does God instruct Moses to lead the Hebrews back to encamp on the shores of the Sea?

10. How does Moses describe God in his hymn of celebration in Exodus 15?

Reading: God Saves His People from Bondage

At the end of the last study we observed how the book of Genesis concludes in a way that anticipates a sequel. The book of Exodus provides that sequel, the action starting perhaps two to four centuries after Joseph. The first verse of Exodus connects back to Genesis. In the first place, Exodus begins with the conjunction "and" (not usually represented in English translations of the book), reminding us that Exodus is a continuation of the story of Genesis. And the rest of the verse repeats Genesis 46:8, reminding us that the origins of Israel in Egypt are found in the descent of Jacob and his family at the time of a severe famine.

But conditions have radically changed since the time Joseph was an important leader in Egypt. The descendants of Abraham have been "exceedingly fruitful," and thus they have "multiplied greatly, increased in numbers and became so numerous that the land was filled with them" (Exodus 1:7). This language should sound familiar after studying Genesis, coming both from the mandate to Adam and Eve to "be fruitful and increase in number; fill the earth and subdue it" (Genesis 1:28) as well as the divine promise to Abraham "I will make you into a great nation" (Genesis 12:2).

On a darker note, the relationship between Egypt and the Israelites has also changed. No longer is it characterized by good will and respect, but now the Egyptians are fearful of Israel and thus oppress them. An unnamed "new king, to whom Joseph meant nothing" (Exodus 1:8) has come to power. He enslaved the Israelites and also issued a command that all the baby boys born to the Hebrews should be put to death.

Who is this "new king," and when do the events of Exodus 1–18 take place? The honest answer is that we do not know. Neither this king nor the king Moses later challenges is mentioned by name. Scholars debate the issue, typically suggesting a time from the exodus itself in either the fifteenth or the thirteenth century B.C., but that is a subject for a different type of study than we are engaged in now (see "Evidence of the Exodus Event," in *How to Read Exodus*).

In this terrifying environment, Moses is born. The story of the midwives appears to answer the question how he survived birth in spite of the Pharaoh's command. The midwives refused to follow through by killing the baby boys and then lied to cover up their actions. The ninth commandment appears to prohibit all lying, but in the light of this story, where God honors the midwives' actions, as well as other stories of lying (for example, Rahab in Joshua 2), it appears that lying is permitted on occasions when the person asking for information wants to use it to harm people (Exodus 1:15-22).

Happily Moses was born without incident, but as he grows older he becomes harder to keep a secret. Moses' mother (elsewhere given the name Jochebed) then places Moses in a papyrus basket (the Hebrew word is the same word used for Noah's ark in Genesis 6:14) coated with tar and pitch. She floats him down the Nile River, where he is discovered by Pharaoh's daughter, who raises him as her own child. She hires Jochebed as the dry nurse, so Moses' mother gets to be with her child and gets paid to do so. The irony of this story is obvious. Pharaoh wants to kill all the baby boys to prevent an uprising of his slaves, but the person God will use to lead their emancipation is raised under his very roof.

While the act of placing Moses in the papyrus basket seems quite unusual to a modern audience, we have at least one other ancient Near Eastern story that is quite similar. In the *Sargon Birth Legend*, the great Akkadian king Sargon describes how his mother, a high priestess, placed him in a basket and floated him down the Euphrates, where he was discovered and raised by an irrigation ditch worker. It appears that Jochebed was acting in a typical fashion when a mother could not keep her child. She was not turning baby Moses over to chance but rather to the care and keeping of God, who would cause the basket to go to safety.

After the account of Moses' birth, the narrative fast-forwards to a story of a grown Moses, who comes to the defense of a fellow Hebrew who was being beaten by an Egyptian (Exodus 2:11-25). In the pro-

cess he killed the Egyptian, and though he thought his deed was done in secret, the next day it becomes clear that his act was public. Accordingly, Moses fled from Egypt to escape punishment. He eventually arrived in Midian, the region occupied by a nomadic sheepherding people located on the Sinai Peninsula as well as the area east of the Gulf of Aqaba. He first encounters some women in distress at a well, whom he helps. One of the women is Zipporah, the daughter of Jethro, whom he marries.

While Moses settles into the life of a shepherd with his new wife and family, God has other plans for him. In one of the most famous scenes in the Bible, Moses sees a bush that was burning but not being consumed by the flames. When he goes to inspect the sight, God speaks to him from the bush.

Why would God choose such a form to make his presence known to Moses? Actually, the burning bush combines two fairly characteristic features of a divine appearance during this early period of biblical history. God appears in fire and smoke elsewhere in the Pentateuch (Genesis 15:17; Exodus 19:18). Fire attracts and fascinates. It is an agent of cleansing, warmth and destruction. Trees and other vegetation also represent God's presence (Genesis 12:6; 13:18, as well as the tree-like lampstand in the tabernacle; Exodus 25:31-40), and a bush is about as close as one can get to a tree in the wilderness. A tree is an image of fertility and life, and God is the author of life.

From the bush God instructs Moses to

return to Egypt in order to rescue the Hebrews from their bondage in Egypt. Moses understandably hesitates, but God assures Moses that he will be with him (Exodus 3:12), language that reminds Moses of the covenant where God promises his people that he will be their God and will be with them.

Nonetheless, Moses still hesitates, anticipating that they will ask for God's name. God responds by revealing his name, Yahweh, which he himself exposits as meaning "I AM WHO I AM" (Exodus 3:14). *Yahweh* often appears in English translations as "the LORD," in order not to offend orthodox Jewish readers who consider it sacrilegious to say God's personal name. The name proclaims that God defines himself. He is the ground of existence.

Moses continues to resist the call, but God gives him signs to perform to bolster his message (Exodus 4:1-9). As we learn from Deuteronomy 18:15-22, a prophet's message must be accompanied by signs that attest to the fact that Yahweh sent him.

Moses hesitates one last time, saying that he was not an eloquent speaker (Exodus 4:10). Eventually, Yahweh makes a concession to Moses by allowing Aaron, Moses' brother, to accompany him as his spokesman.

And off go Moses and his family to Egypt. Some considerable time has passed since Moses fled from Egypt. He not only has a wife and sons, but God tells him that "all those who wanted to kill you are dead" (Exodus 4:19). In the context of their journey to Egypt, a most peculiar event takes place, narrated in one of the admittedly strangest passages in the whole Bible. God attacks Moses to kill him! Zipporah responds by cutting off the foreskin of her son, after which God left Moses alone (Exodus 4:24-26). We are unable to answer all the questions that this enigmatic passage raises in our minds. One thing is crystal clear though. God thinks circumcision is important.

After this, Aaron meets them in the wilderness, and they arrive in Egypt and are well received by the Hebrews, who believe that Moses and Aaron were indeed sent by God to rescue them (Exodus 4:29-31)—at least for the moment.

Moses and Aaron waste no time, and the next scene takes place in the royal court where they demand that Pharaoh "Let my people go" (Exodus 5:1). However, many readers miss the second part of this request. Moses and Aaron do not begin by insisting that Pharaoh free the Hebrew slaves so they can go to the Promised Land. No, they simply ask for a three-day break so they can "journey into the wilderness to offer sacrifices to the LORD our God" (v. 3).

What would the Hebrews have done if Pharaoh had granted their request? We will never know because he adamantly rejects Moses' request. Perhaps he thought that they would not come back, and perhaps they would not have. We have already noted in the episode about the midwives that lying to Pharaoh was not considered evil since Pharaoh was forfeiting the right to the truth because of the harm he was bringing to the people of God. In any case, Pharaoh's refusal also underlines his pettiness and cruelty, a characterization furthered by the fact that he now requires them to make bricks without providing them with straw, which they now had to collect on their own.

When the Hebrews found out that rather than freedom Moses had won them more work, they quickly turned against him (Exodus 5:19-21). Their grumbling against God and Moses begins a pattern that will be repeated countless times through the rest of the Torah, and Moses here responds in a way that becomes typical of him. He turns to God and prays that God will act on his covenant promises.

God responds to Moses' intercession by affirming that he is in control of the situation. He will raise his "mighty hand" against Pharaoh so Pharaoh will not only let them go but will "drive them" from the land (Exodus 6:1). God will do this on the basis of the covenant that he made with Abraham (vv. 2-5; see Genesis 12:1-3).

God's "mighty hand" takes the form of signs and plagues. While these signs and plagues are well known by many Bible readers, it is not as well known that these signs and plagues are acts of war against the gods of the Egyptians. This becomes clear in anticipation of the final plague, the death of the firstborn, when God announces, "On that same night I will pass through Egypt and strike down every firstborn of both people and animals, and I will bring judgment on all the gods of Egypt. I am the LORD" (Exodus 12:12).

In other words, the plagues have the intention of attacking the religious symbolism of the Egyptians. While often opaque to modern readers, there is a reason that the signs and plagues take the form that they do. Let us consider a few examples.

The action begins with Aaron throwing his walking staff to the ground, whereupon it promptly turns into a serpent (Exodus 7:8-13). The serpent was an integral part of Egyptian royal symbolism, since one of the most common crowns has the *uraeus*, a coiled cobra, above the forehead. The coiled cobra was associated with the goddess Wadjet, considered the mother and midwife of the king.

Perhaps surprising to modern readers who tend to think the Egyptian gods were figments of imagination, the priests of Egypt were able to replicate Aaron's act and thus turn their staffs into serpents as well. It is Aaron's one versus the priests' many serpents, but the many are not a match for the one as Aaron's serpent swallows up the serpents produced by the Egyptian wise men.

Where did the Egyptian magicians get the ability to turn their staffs into serpents? We have already seen that God battles the Egyptian gods through these signs and plagues. But these gods are not really gods; they are spiritual powers that we would call demons, who have occupied the religious imaginations of the Egyptians. They have power, but limited power and none in comparison to Yahweh, the God of the Hebrews (see Psalm 106:34-39, where false gods are called demons; see v. 37 [ESV, NASB, NRSV, KJV]).

The contest continues when God turns the waters of the Nile into blood. Now notice that the text says that God turned the water "into blood" (Exodus 7:17), not that he caused the waters to fill up with an unusual amount of reddish algae. I point this out because this plague and indeed all the plagues have been explained by some as natural occurrences and not supernatural interventions, and it is important to realize that the book of Exodus itself does not represent the plagues as natural events.

In any case, the plague of blood is also an attack against a specific Egyptian god. The Egyptians believed that the Nile was represented by a fertility god whom they called Hapi. Imagine the horror of the Egyptians when the Nile, the source of all their fertile land, was blood red. They would think that Hapi had been wounded or worse.

I will give just two more examples of the plagues as attacks on the Egyptian gods. The most important god in Egypt was the sun god, who went by various names, Amun and Re being the most frequent. During the ninth plague, the sun was blotted out. An Egyptian could only think of this as an attack on the all-important god of the sun. But the climax of the plagues comes with the next and last plague, the death of the firstborn. How does this plague attack a god? Pharaoh himself was a god, and the death of his own son would be an attack on that religious idea. God is more powerful than the "gods" of Egypt, more powerful than the god-man Pharaoh, who has presumed

to resist God's command to free his people from their slavery.

Why did Pharaoh resist? Many readers are scandalized to read in Exodus 4:21 that God knew that Pharaoh would resist in spite of the display of God's mighty power in the plagues because God "hardened Pharaoh's heart" (see also Exodus 7:3; 9:12; 10:1, 20, 27; 11:10). Why would God do this? It seems so unfair.

In response, we need to realize that the narrative tells us with equal measure that Pharaoh hardened his own heart (Exodus 8:15, 32; 9:34). In other words, God did not make Pharaoh evil. He is not the author of the harm that Pharaoh's resistance caused to his nation. On the other hand, he doesn't soften Pharaoh's heart either. Why? As difficult as it is for a modern reader to appreciate, the text itself is clear, particularly when it comes to the final hardening just before the crossing of the Sea. God hardens Pharaoh's heart to lead to the final dramatic showdown at the Sea where he will display his awesome glory.

The plague of the firstborn finally broke the Pharaoh's determination to keep the Hebrews as his slaves. He had been warned by God through Moses at the very beginning when God told him, "'Let my son [the Hebrews] go, so he may worship me.' But you refused to let him go; so I will kill your firstborn son" (Exodus 4:23). The enormous importance of this final plague is signaled by the shift in narrative style in Exodus 12 from story to ritual. Exodus 12 establishes an annual festival that continues to be celebrated by Jewish people even today: Passover. Passover commemorates the time when God punished the Hebrews' wicked oppressors but preserved the lives of his oppressed people. Indeed, this event is so momentous that it changed the calendar. From then on, "this month is to be for you the first month, the first month of your year" (Exodus 12:2). Exodus and Passover are forever intertwined, a connection that will be utilized to show that Jesus is even greater than the Passover.

Pharaoh allows the Hebrews to leave. Not only that, but the Lord moved the hearts of the Egyptians so they gave the former slaves gifts of silver and gold as they departed (Exodus 11:1-3). The consequence of receiving these gifts was that the slaves finally got paid for all their hard work! In study 9 we will observe how these metals were used in the construction of the tabernacle in the wilderness.

Freedom at last! God's people are finally heading back to the Promised Land. Reading this story for the first time, we might think that we have reached the end, the hoped-for conclusion. But rescue is not yet complete, since Pharaoh has a change of mind once the slaves have left town. God once again "hardens Pharaoh's heart" with the result that he sets out to reclaim his slaves.

God warns Moses, but rather than placing the Hebrews in a safe place, he actually instructs Moses to lead them to an extremely vulnerable location, at the shores of a large body of water. This sea is often translated as Red Sea, but the Hebrew actually says Reed Sea, and there is some doubt over exactly where it was located. Fortunately, its exact location is not important for the narrative. What we know is that it was a large, impassable body of water. Moses and the Hebrews were in a place where they could not help themselves; they were trapped between the water and an angry and humiliated Pharaoh and his army. By all accounts, they were doomed.

But God placed the Hebrews there to demonstrate his glory by dramatically saving his people and punishing the Egyptians, as they deserved. As Moses raised his walking stick, God parted the waters and allowed his people to escape, and as the Egyptians followed, God closed the waters on top of them. Thus God's people are freed from Egypt and begin their trek toward the Promised Land (see study 7).

Exodus 15 records one of the most famous songs in the entire Bible, Moses' song celebrating God's great victory over Egypt at the Reed Sea. Here the Israelites praise God for being their "warrior" and fighting on their behalf against their cruel and oppressive enemies. It also looks forward to the future battle against the inhabitants of the Promised Land. They too are more powerful than Israel, but God will exert his power and bring them into the land. God, after all, is their powerful king (Exodus 15:18).

Reading Study Guide

1. How is the opening of the book of Exodus connected to the ending of the book of Genesis?

2. Why did Pharaoh fear the Israelites?

3. Do you think it was right for the midwives to lie to Pharaoh about the birth of Hebrew babies? Why or why not?

4. What is ironic about the story of Moses' birth?

5. At the burning bush God reveals his proper name—Yahweh (usually translated "the LORD" in English). What is the significance of this name (Exodus 3)?

6. What is meant by the fact that God hardened Pharaoh's heart?

Do you think this was fair? Why or why not?

7. Read Exodus 12 again. What are Israelite families supposed to do to commemorate the Passover?

8. How is God glorified through the events at the Reed Sea?

9. Moses describes God as a warrior in Exodus 15:3. What is your reaction to the picture of God as a warrior who fights and destroys the Egyptian army?

Anticipating the New Testament

The exodus event was remembered as the most important salvation event of the Old Testament period. As such, it brought comfort to people who struggled with trouble. Psalm 77 is a lament of a person who is in deep distress (vv. 1-9). He thought that his life was beyond rescue. That is, until he looked to the past and thought about God's mighty acts of redemption. In particular, he remembers the crossing of the Sea (vv. 16-20). At that time, the Israelites were beyond any hope of rescue, but God opened the Sea for them. This remembrance gives the psalmist confidence to live in midst of a troubled present and hope for the future.

Strikingly, prophets who live many centuries after the exodus speak about the exodus not as a past event but as a future one. Two examples are Isaiah 4:1-5 and Hosea 2:14-15 (both in the eighth century B.C., some four to seven centuries after the exodus), both of whom see a second exodus following a time when God will judge Israel for its sins.

The Gospel of Mark opens by quoting Isaiah and anticipates the fulfillment of his prophecy of the fulfillment of the exodus (Mark 1:1-3). Jesus is that fulfillment, and his life follows the pattern of the exodus and wilderness wandering. His baptism is equivalent to Israel's Sea crossing (see 1 Corinthians 10:1-6), followed by forty days and nights in the wilderness where he experienced the same temptations (hunger, testing God and the worship of a false god) that Israel experienced in the wilderness. Jesus, though, is the obedient son of God in contrast to the disobedient children of Israel. Many other parallels occur, and they climax with his crucifixion on the eve of Passover, the festival of the exodus. Jesus is "our Passover lamb."

1. What is the significance of the parallels between Jesus and the exodus?

2. The psalmist looked back to the past, specifically the exodus, to gain, confidence and hope in a troubled present. How might our understanding that Jesus' ministry fulfills the exodus affect the way Christians read and apply Psalm 77 in our lives?

 The Ancient Story and Our Story

AN EXODUS FROM SIN AND DEATH

By any standard, the story of the exodus is a dramatic and inspiring account of liberation from bondage, in which the Israelites are freed from their slavery in Egypt. God freed them from Egypt and bound them to himself. Their freedom is found in serving the true King, Yahweh.

We can see how this account became a favorite of slaves in the period before the Civil War, as well as other oppressed people who find hope of liberation in this narrative. But how does it speak to most of us who are reading this book? We have never been slaves . . . or have we?

Paul describes life before turning to Christ as slavery, bondage to sin and to death (Romans 6). All of us have been there, and perhaps some who read this book still are enslaved to sin and the fear of death. In other words, those who are slaves of sin and death are controlled by these destructive forces. Paul, though, tells Christians that thanks to Jesus "we are no longer slaves to sin. For when we died with Christ we were set free from the power of sin" (Romans 6:6-7 NLT). Paul goes on to tell us that this has very important implications for how we live, "Do not let sin control the way you live; do not give in to sinful desires" (Romans 6:12 NLT). In other words, the struggle still continues; even after we become Christians, we are still tempted to sin. Paul recounts that struggle in chapter 7 (read Romans 7:7-25). Where does Paul find the solution to this internal struggle? "The answer is in Jesus Christ our Lord" (Roman 7:25 NLT). Jesus gives us the power to resist sin. We need to proclaim our freedom from slavery to sin and death and give ourselves "to be slaves to righteous living so that you will become holy" (Romans 6:19 NLT).

GOD SAVES WHEN LIFE IS OUT OF CONTROL

The exodus, and particularly the crossing of the Sea, demonstrates that God can save his people when they have no resources to save themselves. We often find ourselves in predicaments that are beyond our capacity to resolve. Perhaps we or someone we love is dealing with an addiction. Or maybe we have a financial obligation that we can't meet or a disease that has no cure. How does the account of the exodus speak to us in these moments of our life? It reminds us that God can rescue us when we can't rescue ourselves. It engenders hope in our life, when our natural tendency is to slide into despair in our helplessness.

Does this mean that God will always "open up the sea" so we can get beyond our problems? Not necessarily in this life. But we know that our death does not end the story. Our Promised Land is not Canaan but heaven itself. No matter what our present issue, we know that God can solve it now, but if in his wisdom he does not, we know that our future is secure.

LOOKING AHEAD

The story of the exodus began with Israel living as slaves in Egypt, but at the end of the story, they are free from the Egyptians and living in relationship (as servants) with Yahweh. They are heading to the land of promise, but to reach the land, they have to traverse the wilderness where they will experience trials and temptations and ultimately the judgment of God (see study 7).

Going Deeper

Enns, Peter. *Exodus*. NIV Application Commentary. Grand Rapids: Zondervan, 2000.

Longman, Tremper, III. *How to Read Exodus*. Downers Grove, IL: InterVarsity Press, 2009.

7 / Wilderness Wandering

LOOKING AHEAD

MEMORY VERSE: Hebrews 3:18-19
BIBLE STUDY: Exodus 16; 32; Numbers 1–2; 13–14; 20:1-13; 24–26; Deuteronomy 1:1-8; 34
READING: God Refines His People

 ## Bible Study Guide

After reading Exodus 16; 32; Numbers 1–2; 13–14; 20:1-13; 24–26; Deuteronomy 1:1-8; 34, spend some time reflecting on these passages with the following questions in mind before looking at the Reading. (For maximum benefit read Exodus 15:22–Deuteronomy 34:12.)

1. Exodus 16 records events soon after God's great act of rescue at the Red Sea. How would you characterize Israel's attitude at this time?

   What one word repeated in this chapter indicates that attitude?

2. Exodus 32 describes the sin of the golden calf, which occurs right after God gives instructions to build the tabernacle (Exodus 25–31). We will study this passage more carefully in study 9, but what does this chapter tell us about Israel's relationship with God?

3. Numbers 1 provides a census of men who are "twenty years old or more and able to serve in the army" (Numbers 1:3). Why do you think only men over twenty are counted?

4. Read Numbers 1:53–2:34. Draw a diagram showing where the Levites and the other tribes place their tents relative to the tabernacle.

5. Why does God condemn the Israelites to spend forty years in the wilderness (Numbers 13–14)?

6. According to Numbers 22, Balak, king of Moab, hires Balaam to curse Israel as they pass through his land. Read Numbers 24 and describe what he says about Israel.

7. How does Moab almost destroy Israel according to Numbers 25, and how does Israel deal with the threat?

8. In Numbers 26, we have a second census (see Numbers 1). Are they counting the same people?

9. Where is Israel when Moses delivers his last sermon, which is now recorded in the book of Deuteronomy (Deuteronomy 1:1-8; 34)?

👓 Reading: God Refines His People

When the Israelites were freed from Egyptian bondage, they had a destination, the Promised Land, the land from which Jacob and his family came to flee the horrible famine that struck Canaan (see study 5). The distance was not far, and though they had a planned stop at Mount Sinai, Deuteronomy 1:2 tells us that "it takes eleven days to go from Horeb [another name for Mount Sinai] to Kadesh Barnea," and it was not a long distance to the southern portion of the Promised Land from there. However, rather than a few days or weeks or months, they spent forty years in the wilderness between Egypt and Canaan. We read about these years in the books of Exodus, Leviticus, Numbers and Deuteronomy.

The first phase of the wilderness period involves the trek from the Sea to Mount Sinai, the place God prearranged with Moses to come so he could make his presence known in a dramatic way to his people there.

Right from the start, there was trouble. They traveled for three days without finding water (Exodus 15:22-27). Now, God had just delivered them from the Egyptian army at the Red Sea, but still they could not maintain trust in their God. Rather than moving on in faith, the Israelites "grumbled" against Moses. Here we have the first occurrence of a word that will reverberate through the texts that narrate the wilderness wanderings. Grumbling indicates deep dissatisfaction and simmering anger. This anger is directed toward Moses, but Moses is God's representative to them and soon we will see that they are not hesitant to express their anger toward God directly.

Eventually, the Israelites discovered water, but the water was bitter, that is, undrinkable. They even named the place Marah, which means "bitter." God showed Moses a piece of wood that when thrown into the water made it drinkable. God once again shows himself reliable, providing for the people in the wilderness. He uses this occasion to warn them to be very careful to obey him.

Even so, as the story continues in Exodus 16, the people continue their grumbling. This time they complain about a lack of food. They are hungry, but rather than turning toward God in faith to provide, they rather wish they had never left Egypt.

God responds to their need by providing them with manna, a name which comes from a Hebrew phrase "What is it?" (Exodus 16:15). While there are theories, we know about as much as the Israelites as to the nature of the manna. The manna appeared on the ground six days a week (not on the sabbath; they were to collect twice as much the day before), and "it was white like coriander seed and tasted like wafers made with honey" (Exodus 16:31). In addition to the manna, God also provided quail for them to eat.

Still, the people were not done with

their grumbling. They were thirsty again and threatened Moses. God responds by telling Moses to use his walking stick to hit a rock, which then flowed with water. The names given to the location of this provision of water are telling. They are called Massah, which means "testing," and Meribah, which means "quarreling."

Soon the Israelites arrive at Mount Sinai, the place near which God had earlier revealed himself to Moses at the burning bush to commission him to go to Egypt (Exodus 3). God made his presence known to Israel at Mount Sinai, and it was here that God gave Moses the Ten Commandments and the law (Exodus 19–24). Further, he also instructed Moses to build the tabernacle, giving them the pattern for its construction (Exodus 25–40). These events are so important that I have devoted the next two chapters to the law (study 8) and to the tabernacle (study 9, which also looks at the priesthood and sacrifices). Still, at this point it is important, as we consider the spiritual attitude of the people, to recognize that even at this most holy moment the people find occasion to sin, and sin greatly. While Moses is on Mount Sinai receiving the law and the instructions to build the tabernacle, the people under the leadership of Aaron construct an idol, a golden calf (Exodus 32).

Thus when Moses returns from the mountain and sees their idolatry, he smashes the tablets of the law, reflecting a broken relationship with God. Indeed, God wants to destroy the people and start all over. But Moses intercedes on their behalf and restores relationship with God, so God agrees to continue to move with them through the wilderness. He makes his presence known through a cloud. When the tabernacle is finished, the cloud fills the building. But when God wants them to march, he guides them with a pillar of cloud by day that has fire in it by night (Exodus 40:34-38).

The Israelites spend a little less than a year camped at Mount Sinai as they build the tabernacle and ready themselves for the rest of the journey. This period of time also constitutes a large portion of the wilderness narrative in the Bible (Exodus 19:1–Numbers 10:10). Much of this material is devoted to law and the building of the tabernacle; the march begins again in Numbers 10:11 as they head to the Promised Land.

The book of Numbers describes the transition from Sinai to the plains of Moab. The book opens at Sinai and closes at Moab, right across from the Promised Land. It is on the plains of Moab that Moses delivers his final sermon that we know as the book of Deuteronomy. It is from the plains of Moab that Joshua will cross the Jordan River and begin the conquest of the land.

Numbers also tells us why it took forty years and not a matter of days to travel from Sinai to the Promised Land. The book begins with what looks like a census, but it is really more like a military registration, counting men over twenty who are ready for war. This chapter is the first hint that the book of Numbers views Israel, as it marches through the wilderness, as not a ragtag group but rather an army on the march. Numbers 1:53—2:34 underlines this idea as it depicts the layout of the wilderness camp. Here we see that the tabernacle, representing God's dwelling on earth, is in the center immediately surrounded by the Levites. Then the rest of the tribes are positioned to the east, west, south and north of the tabernacle. To one aware of ancient Near Eastern customs, it is obvious that the camp follows the model of a war camp. The war leader, in this case God, has his tent in the middle of the camp, surrounded by his bodyguard (for priests as bodyguards of God's holiness, see study 9), and then the rest of the army. Interestingly, and carrying even further the idea that Israel in the wilderness is pictured as an army on the march, notice what Moses proclaims whenever Israel breaks camp and begins to march:

Rise up, LORD!
    May your enemies be scattered;
    may your foes flee before you.
        (Numbers 10:35)

God the warrior (see study 10) leads his army through the wilderness toward the Promised Land.

However, Israel's march turns out to be anything but triumphant. We have already noted that right from the start Israel's relationship with God was deeply problematic. They grumbled and complained every step of the way. They tested God and rebelled against him. The book of Numbers adds more stories of Israel's troubled relationship with God.

Space only permits a sampling of some of the more egregious examples, the first being Miriam and Aaron's complaints about Moses' privileged position (Numbers 12). Their jealousy compelled them to question Moses' authority, using his marriage to a Cushite as pretense. The precise nature of their issue with Moses' marriage escapes us, but God recognizes that it is an attack on his preeminent position in Israel, and the Lord speaks strongly to reaffirm his leadership role:

When there is a prophet among you,
    I, the LORD, reveal myself to them
        in visions,
    I speak to them in dreams.
But this is not true of my servant
        Moses;
    he is faithful in all my house.
With him I speak face to face,
    clearly and not in riddles;
    he sees the form of the LORD.
Why then were you not afraid
    to speak against my servant Moses?
        (Numbers 12:6-8)

Aaron and Miriam were not the only ones who questioned Moses' leadership. Korah, a Levite, and two men from the tribe of Reuben, Dathan and Abiram, also led a revolt against Moses. God responded to this threat by opening up the ground under the rebels and sending fire to consume them (Numbers 16).

Numbers 17 narrates an attack on Aaron's authority. Aaron had been appointed high priest by God, but the other tribal leaders questioned this choice. God told them all to place their walking staffs before him. Aaron's preferential status was confirmed when God caused his staff to blossom like an almond tree.

However, the episode that consigned Israel to spend the next forty years in the wilderness is narrated in Numbers 13–14 and concerns a spy mission to the Promised Land. While at Kadesh Barnea, Moses commissioned twelve spies, one from each tribe, to go up into the Promised Land and report back. When they returned, they had a classic good news-bad news report. The good news was that this was a land of "milk and honey," in other words a fertile and luxurious land. The bad news was "the land we explored devours those living in it. All the people we saw there are of great size. We saw the Nephilim there (the descendants of Anak come from the Nephilim). We seemed like grasshoppers in our own eyes, and we looked the same to them" (Numbers 13:32-33).

This report sent shivers down the spines of the Israelites. Among the spies only two men, Joshua and Caleb, had faith that no matter how formidable the inhabitants of the land, God was able to defeat them. After all, God had demonstrated his power against the Egyptians at the Red Sea and now dwelled in their midst as the war leader of Israel. They should have realized that they were an army on the march, and since God was with them, they could defeat any enemy.

It was this complete lack of trust that led God to decree that the generation that came up out of Egypt would die in the wilderness, never seeing the Promised Land. The only exceptions would be Joshua and Caleb. Israel would wander for forty years, enough time for that generation (twenty years old and older) to die off.

Hearing this, the Israelites panicked once again. This time they garnered their courage and attacked the gigantic inhabitants of the Promised Land. However, God had already made his decision, and they were soundly defeated. When they returned, disheartened, they knew that they would die in the wilderness.

Moses too would have been exempt from this sentence of death. However, Numbers 20:1-13 relates the event that led to Moses' exclusion from the land. On surface reading, Moses' offense seems slight. The people are again complaining about a lack of water. Moses and Aaron are obviously irritated with them, but God tells them to speak to the rock and the rock would flow with water (similarly to the account in Exodus 17:1-7). However, notice what Moses actually does. When he appears before the people, rather than giving the glory to God, he says, "Listen, you rebels, must we bring you water out of this rock?" (v. 10). In other words, he implicitly claims that it is he and Aaron, not God, who provide them with water. But then, rather than speaking to the rock, he hits it (out of anger) with his staff. Though it is not clearly stated, the rock probably represents God (see also 1 Corinthians 10:1-6). Because of Moses and Aaron's actions here, they will not be permitted to enter the land.

Eventually, though, the Israelites leave

Kadesh Barnea and begin to move toward the Promised Land. In the Transjordan region (on the east of the Jordan River), they are denied passage by Sihon king of the Amorites and Og king of Bashan (Numbers 21:21-35). Israel soundly defeats them and possesses their land. A potentially more serious obstacle came in the form of the Moabites, whose king also did not want them to pass through their land. He went so far as to hire a diviner to curse the Israelites as they pass through.

Modern readers know Balaam mostly because of his donkey. Each time he tried to leave to fulfill his mission and collect his pay, his donkey would refuse to move. Finally, as Balaam was beating it, the donkey spoke and informed him that his way was being blocked by nothing less than the angel of the Lord.

God is in control, and he tells Balaam that he can only speak words that he, God, gives to him. These are words of blessing not curse, including the dramatic words that anticipate the rise of kingship in Israel:

> I see him, but not now;
>   I behold him, but not near.
> A star will come out of Jacob;
>   a scepter will rise out of Israel.
> He will crush the foreheads of Moab,
>   the skulls of all the people of
>   Sheth.
> Edom will be conquered;
>   Seir, his enemy, will be
>   conquered,
>   but Israel will grow strong.
> A ruler will come out of Jacob

and destroy the survivors of the city. (Numbers 24:17-19)

Needless to say, Balak was upset and Balaam unpaid. However, the next chapter shows that Balaam found another way to accomplish his goal, or nearly so. He was the one who devised the plan (see Numbers 31:16) to send beautiful Moabite women to seduce Israel and to lead them to worship their false gods. Israel was saved by the quick action of Phinehas, a priestly descendant of Aaron, who defended God's holiness by killing an Israelite and his Moabite lover (Numbers 25:7-8).

After the account of Balaam and the Moabites, Numbers gives us a second census, again more accurately described as a military registration. Looking closely, we see that this census counts the second generation rather than the first generation and thus marks the transition to the people who will actually enter the land. Indeed, after Numbers 26, we do not hear of any more grumbling or difficulties.

Thus Israel, the second generation, arrives at the plains of Moab, the staging area for entry into the Promised Land (Deuteronomy 1:1-8). The book of Deuteronomy contains Moses' final words to Israel. He is speaking now to the generation that will enter the Promised Land, and he leads them in a reaffirmation of the covenant that they entered with God at Mount Sinai. And once they do so, Moses ascends Mount Nebo, from which he could see far into the Promised Land, where he will die without entering the land.

Thus ends the period of the wilderness wanderings, a period prolonged because of the sin of the people. The wilderness is the place where those who were over twenty at the time of the exodus died, to be succeeded by their children, now adults ready to go into the land. The wilderness was a place of testing and refinement, preparing Israel for what was to come.

Reading Study Guide

1. The first generation of Israelites who left Egypt constantly grumbled and complained about the conditions of their life in the wilderness. Do you have sympathy for them? Why or why not?

2. God condemned the Israelites to spend the next forty years in the wilderness, the time it would take for the first generation of Israelites to leave Egypt to die. What was the occasion for God to issue this decree?

   Do you think this occasion was the only reason God judged them in this way?

3. What is the significance of the cloud during the wilderness wanderings?

4. Why is it appropriate to consider Israel in the wilderness as an "army on the march"?

   Does this change your understanding of this period of Israel's history?

5. What is the significance and relationship of the two "census" accounts (really military registrations) in Numbers 1 and 26?

6. What frightened the Israelites about the spies' report after they returned from the Promised Land (Numbers 13–14)?

Why was their fear misplaced?

7. Why were Moses and Aaron not permitted to enter the Promised Land?

Do you think their punishment was fair? Why or why not?

8. Read Jude 11 and discuss what motivated Balaam to continue to look for ways to destroy Israel even though God kept him from cursing them.

⮕ Anticipating the New Testament

In study 6 on the exodus we saw how the prophets of the Old Testament began to talk about a future exodus and wilderness wandering (Hosea 2:14-15; Isaiah 40:1-5), and that the Gospel writers recognized that these hopes were being fulfilled in Jesus Christ, whose ministry began with his baptism in the wilderness area by John the Baptist, followed by forty days and forty nights where he experienced the same temptations that Israel did in the wilderness. However, though Israel succumbed to the temptations, Jesus remained obedient. It was most convenient to cover these texts in conjunction with the exodus, but they are also relevant for how the wilderness wandering narrative anticipates the coming of Christ.

1. Think about a wilderness you find yourself in now or in the past. How can it encourage you to connect your wilderness experience to the coming of Christ?

The Ancient Story and Our Story

The author of Hebrews draws on Israel's wilderness experience to drive home the crucial point that his Christian readers must be on guard against unbelief and disobedience. We all have a propensity to go on "cruise control" in our relationship with God. We become too busy and distracted, and our spiritual growth gets stunted and our relationship with God may eventually die.

We also have the same tendency to grumble and complain about God like Israel did in the wilderness. There is nothing wrong with complaining *to* God, as we will learn from the laments in the book of Psalms (see study 13), but it is a whole different thing to complain *about* God. The latter indicates that we have no real hope that God hears our prayers and does something about them. We marvel that Israel can grumble and lose hope in God in the wilderness so soon after God had just delivered them from Egypt, the most powerful nation on the face of the earth. But then, if we think about it, we too have been saved from an even stronger power, the power of sin and death, by Jesus, who died and was raised on the cross, yet we still find ourselves dissatisfied with life.

Hebrews speaks to Christians to tell them that we are in exactly the same place as the wilderness wanderers (Hebrews 3:7–4:13). They had been saved from Egypt; we have been saved from sin and death. They were heading to the Promised Land; we are heading to heaven. However, in the present we are in the wilderness.

The author of Hebrews then reminds us that the first generation rebelled in the wilderness and therefore died. He reminds us that in this life we are pilgrims in the wilderness and we need to maintain our faith or we will die and not enter the sabbath rest God has reserved for us. To make his point, he cites Psalm 95 and applies it to Christians:

> Today, if you hear his voice,
> > do not harden your hearts
> as you did in the rebellion,
> > during the time of testing in the wilderness,
> where your ancestors tested and tried me,
> > though for forty years they saw what I did.
> That is why I was angry with that generation;
> > I said, "Their hearts are always going astray,
> > and they have not known my ways."
> So I declared on oath in my anger,
> > "They shall never enter my rest." (Hebrews 3:7-11)

Thus, the story of the wilderness wanderings reminds us that we are pilgrims in this world and we need to remain faithful in order to enter our true home.

LOOKING AHEAD

The wilderness wandering covers the period from the exodus up to the eve of the conquest. Due to Israel's sin, they stayed in the wilderness forty years, until the first generation died off. Now they are prepared to go into the Promised Land and conquer their enemies. Before we look at the conquest (study 10), we will take a closer look at the law (study 8) and the worship institutions (priests, holy places and sacrifices) that originated during the wilderness period (study 9).

Going Deeper

Gane, Roy. *Leviticus, Numbers*. NIV Application Commentary. Grand Rapids: Zondervan, 2004.

8 / Law

LOOKING AHEAD

MEMORY VERSE: Psalm 119:1-8
BIBLE STUDY: Exodus 19–24
READING: God Makes His Will Known

 **Bible Study Guide**

After reading Exodus 19–24, spend some time reflecting on this passage with the following questions in mind before looking at the Reading. (For all the law see also Leviticus 1–7; 11–27; Numbers 5:1–10:10; 15; 18–19; 28–30; Deuteronomy 4–28.)

1. What do you think the relationship between law and grace is during the Old Testament period of time?

2. How did the Israelites break the first commandment to worship the Lord alone?

   How do people in modern society break the commandment?

3. What does it mean to make an "image" of God (Exodus 20:4-6)?

4. How does one "misuse" the name of God and thus break the third commandment (Exodus 20:7)?

5. The fourth commandment (Exodus 20:8-11) says to observe the sabbath, the seventh day of the week (Friday sundown until Saturday sundown). Why do most Christians treat Sunday as the Lord's Day?

6. How can children show "honor" to their parents (Exodus 20:12)?

   Is this the same as to obey one's parents?

7. Does the sixth commandment (Exodus 20:13) prohibit all killing? Explain.

8. What makes the tenth commandment ("you must not covet" [Exodus 20:17]) different from the first nine commandments?

9. Why do many Christians observe the Ten Commandments, but not the law (the case law) that follows them (Exodus 20:22–23:19)?

Reading: God Makes His Will Known

After leaving Egypt, Moses led Israel to Mount Sinai, where they had a pre-arranged meeting with the God who had rescued them from their slavery. God had given them their freedom from their Egyptian overlords, but not so they could be completely independent of all authority. Indeed, now they were servants of a new king—Yahweh himself, and at Mount Sinai he would reveal his law to his people. Of course, it was one thing to be a slave of Egypt and another to be a servant of Yahweh, who loved and wanted his best for his people.

Now, of course, God had always let his people know his will. They knew God did not want them to murder, commit adultery, lie, worship foreign gods and so on well before he gave Moses the two tablets of stone. Indeed, Abraham, who lived many centuries before Moses, was described in Genesis as someone who "did everything I required of him, keeping my commands, my decrees and my instructions" (Genesis 26:5). But now the people of God were more than an extended family; they were God's nation. As a nation, the law took a more formal shape as the Ten Commandments and the case laws that derive from those commandments.

The law was not given in a vacuum but rather in the context of a relationship with God, which is defined by the covenant. *Covenant* is a term that describes a legal relationship. Scholars have noticed that the biblical idea of covenant resembles ancient Near Eastern treaties, particularly those in which a king of a superpower enters into a relationship with a lesser kingdom. Of course, in these biblical covenants, God is the great king who enters into a treaty relationship with the Israelites, who occupy the place of the lesser power.

For the purposes of understanding Old Testament law, the most important implication is that law is given in the context of an already established gracious relationship between God and Israel. In other words, grace precedes law. It is commonplace to say that the Old Testament is a religion of law while the New Testament is a religion of grace, but this is not true. In ancient Near Eastern treaties, which are the background of the biblical idea of the covenant, law comes after the so-called historical prologue, which recounts the good deeds that the superior nation's king had done for the less powerful king.

While the human treaties of the ancient Near East may be just so much political propaganda, God truly did establish a loving relationship with his people *before* he gave them his law. We can observe this in the short preamble that introduces the Ten Commandments: "I am the LORD your God, who brought you out of Egypt, out of the land of slavery" (Exodus 20:2).

The law itself can be divided into two main types. First, already mentioned, we have the Ten Commandments (Exodus

20:3-17), followed by numerous other laws that are often called case laws, for reasons soon to be explained. This structure is also found in the book of Deuteronomy, which contains an even longer section on law. After a historical prologue that details how good God has treated Israel (Deuteronomy 1:9–3:29), we find again the Ten Commandments (Deuteronomy 5:7-21), followed by a very long section of case law (Deuteronomy 6–26). This section is significantly followed by a list of blessings and curses contingent on obedience or disobedience to the law. Ancient Near Eastern treaties also have such sanctions.

To truly understand the nature of biblical law, we must recognize the relationship between the Ten Commandments and the case law that follows them. For purposes of illustration, we will focus in on the law found in Exodus 20–24.

Of course, the Ten Commandments are among the best-known portions of the Old Testament, though most people cannot name all ten. What makes them unique not only in relationship to biblical law, but also to other ancient Near Eastern law, is that they are expressed in the form of universal ethical principles. Case law, we will see, addresses a specific situation. As I will illustrate later, the case law is actually an application of the general ethical principles of the Ten Commandments to a particular situation.

But first I make some observations about the Ten Commandments as a whole and then about each of the individual commandments.

The Ten Commandments may be divided into two main parts. The first four commandments concern Israel's relationship with God, and then the final six commandments deal with humans' relationships with other humans.

The first commandment is the most fundamental of all. "You shall have no other gods before me" (Exodus 20:3). Yahweh demands exclusive worship. He may not be replaced or supplemented by other gods. This commandment is quite radical in its ancient Near Eastern context since all other nations worshiped not one but many gods and goddesses. Notice that the commandment insists on sole worship of Yahweh, even if there are other gods! Remember from the study of the exodus (study 6) that the plagues were envisioned as a battle against the Egyptian gods over whom God won victory during the final plague (Exodus 12:12). The worship of false gods becomes a serious problem for Israel and leads eventually to the destruction of Jerusalem, according to the prophets.

The second commandment prohibits the manufacture of images or idols for the purpose of worshiping them. Like the first commandment, the prohibition of idols was unique in the ancient Near Eastern world, where all the gods were represented by statues that were covered in precious metals, were fed and taken on processions through the city streets. Israel will demonstrate its propensity toward idol worship as early as Exodus 32, where they bow the knee to a golden calf. Debate continues over exactly how far this prohibition reaches. While some people think it means that there should be no artistic representation of God, others rightly suggest that it forbids only artistic representations that lead to worship of the object itself.

The third commandment condemns the "misuse" of God's name. The commandment is purposefully vague because there are many different ways of misusing God's name. God's name might be used to curse something out of personal vengeance, or evoked in a false oath or vow. The commandment might also be broken by using God's name in a flippant way, OMG. Conservative Jews take a radical step in order to obey this commandment. They never speak God's name. However, though the commandment prohibits a misuse of God's name, it certainly does not discourage the praise of his name, and the psalms, among other places, invite God's people to extol the name of God (Psalm 7:17; 9:2; 22:22).

The fourth commandment, and the last one that directly concerns relationship with God, concerns the sabbath. The commandment prohibits regular work during the seventh day of the week, grounding the observance of the sabbath in the creation week where God worked six days and rested on the seventh. We cannot overestimate the importance of the sabbath during the Old Testament period since it was considered the "sign" of the Mosaic covenant of law (Exodus 31:12-18).

The first of the commandments that focus on human-human relationships is the command to "honor" father and mother. Like with the third commandment, the verb *honor* is vague and makes us wonder exactly what it means to honor one's parents. We almost expect to see "obey" rather than "honor," but God well knew that some ungodly parents should not be obeyed, though they should be honored rather than ignored or worse.

The sixth commandment prohibits "murder." It is important to note that not all killing is considered wrong in the Old Testament. After all, the law itself mandates capital punishment for some crimes. In addition, through the Old Testament, God sometimes commands Israel to go to battle. However, the illegitimate taking of life was forbidden.

The seventh commandment condemns adultery. Adultery is sexual intercourse outside of marriage. As is typical, the case law will identify specific cases that would be considered adulterous and even names certain types of relationships where neither marriage nor sex is permitted (Leviticus 18; 20). Adultery assumes that marriage is an exclusive relationship between husbands and wives. While it is true that during the biblical period a man was permitted to have more than one wife, sexual intercourse was only permitted within the context of the legal relationship known as marriage.

The eighth commandment protects private property by forbidding theft. The case law shows by the less intense penalties associated with stealing that people are more important than property, but the law clearly recognizes the concept of ownership.

The ninth commandment forbids "false testimony against your neighbor." This law uses the language of the courtroom, where truth is vital. After all, in an age before forensic evidence, trials depended on eyewitness testimony. That is why a later case law requires two witnesses for a case that involves the death penalty (Numbers 35:30). Though the law specifies the courtroom, it would apply more broadly to lying in general. However, as we saw in the case of the midwives in Exodus 1, there do appear to be certain circumstances when lying was not only acceptable but right.

The tenth and final commandment is significantly different than the first nine and deeply influences our understanding of all the commandments. In its prohibition of coveting, this law internalizes all the other commandments. One not only should refrain from adultery but also from coveting (lusting after) a man or a woman who is not one's spouse. One should not only refrain from killing but also from hating a person so much that one would want to kill them. Jesus later reasserts this true understanding of the commandments over against the contemporary teachers of the law who externalized the commandments when he said, "You have heard that it was said to the people long ago, 'You shall not murder, and anyone who murders will be subject to judgment.' But I tell you that anyone who is angry with a brother or sister will be subject to judgment" (Matthew 5:21-22; see Matthew 5:27-28 for adultery).

These are the Ten Commandments. Their importance is underlined by the fact that they appear first among the laws in both Exodus 19–24 as well as Deuteronomy 5–26. However, there are many other laws that follow the Ten Commandments, which we know of as case laws because they describe specific instances of breaking the law. The Ten Commandments provide the legal-ethical principles that are then applied to specific situations in the case law. A quick example comes from Exodus 22:1: "Whoever steals an ox or a sheep and slaughters it or sells it must pay back five head of cattle for the ox and four sheep for the sheep." This law, of course, is an application of the eighth commandment, "You shall not steal," to the case of one's livestock. The case law also usually addresses the question of penalty for infraction of the law as well, a subject we will return to momentarily.

So the main difference between the Ten Commandments and the case law is that the former are general ethical principles and the latter applies these general principles to specific situations. A further important observation is that the specific situations envisioned by the case laws are connected to the sociological and redemptive historical condition of the people of God at the time. In terms of sociological condition, the law addresses a nonurban, pastoral people. To speak of redemptive history is simply to say that the law addresses God's people before the coming of Christ. As we will observe later, the coming of Christ does affect how Christians apply the law to themselves.

Let's take a couple of examples to illustrate. The goring ox law (Exodus 21:28-36) shows that the case law is shaped to speak to the needs of ancient Israelites' sociological condition. The general ethical principle is the commandment "You shall not murder" and is applied to the question of who is responsible for damages and death perpetrated by a person's animals. If the ox gores someone once, the animal must be destroyed. If it is not destroyed and the animal gores another person, then the owner himself is subject to the death penalty.

In the second place, the case law addresses Israel at its particular redemptive historical moment. The most obvious place where this affects our understanding of the law has to do with what today is called ceremonial law, those laws that speak to Israel's worship. In Exodus 19–24 there are a limited number of ceremonial laws (though see Exodus 23:10-19); the laws in Numbers, Leviticus and Deuteronomy contain many that concern Israel's place of worship, its priests, its time of worship and its method of worship (particularly sacrifice). Later we will observe how the coming of Christ radically changes our use of these laws.

Before turning to the New Testament, though, I need to comment on the penalties of the law. Many laws state the penalty that comes with breaking the law. We have already seen that the ox law mandates the owner's death if the animal gores someone a second time. Before that we observed that someone who stole an animal would have to provide restitution. While on first reading, the Old Testament law seems quite severe since many of the provisions call for the death penalty, Numbers 35:31-32 suggests that in most instances the death penalty was a maximum penalty. To insist that death is the one and only penalty for murder implies that the judge and perhaps the victim could allow for a lesser penalty for other crimes.

In this essay, we have put our focus on understanding the Old Testament law in its Old Testament context. Law is based on grace. The Ten Commandments articulate general ethical principles that are applied to specific situations in the case law according to the sociological and redemptive-historical context of the people of God, Israel, at the time. Penalties accompanied the laws and were often quite severe. In the next part of the study, we will consider how a Christian should view the Old Testament law.

Reading Study Guide

1. What is the difference between being a slave to Egypt and a servant of God?

2. What role does the law have in the formation of Israel as a nation?

3. Describe the relationship between law and grace in the Old Testament.

4. What is the relationship between covenant and treaty? How does law fit into the picture?

5. What is the relationship between the Ten Commandments and the case law? Give examples.

6. Read Exodus 22:16-24. How do these case laws relate to the Ten Commandments?

7. Read Leviticus 18, which forbids sex and marriage for certain types of relationships. What are these relationships?

8. Do people today make idols and thus break the second commandment? If so, how?

9. Name the Ten Commandments in their proper order.

10. Is lying always wrong? If so, what about the midwives who lie to Pharaoh (Exodus 1:15-21) or Rahab who lies to the king of Jericho (Joshua 2)?

⟳ Anticipating the New Testament

Jesus strongly affirms the continuing importance of the Old Testament law (Matthew 5:17-20). On the other hand, the New Testament also makes clear that his life, death and resurrection radically affect how the Christian views and observes the law.

A number of Old Testament laws concern rituals that speak to the time (sabbath and festivals), the human agents (priests), the actions (sacrifice) and the place (tabernacle and temple) of worship. These are called ceremonial laws. Jesus fulfills these ceremonial laws. He is the once-and-for-all sacrifice (Hebrews 10:1-18), the ultimate high priest (Hebrews 9:11-28), the presence of God that renders symbolic representations of God's presence like the sanctuary unnecessary (John 1:14). In the Old Testament period there was a need for designated holy time, people, actions and places. Now all time, all people, all actions and all places are holy. We can all worship in God's presence anytime and anyplace (Colossians 2:16-17).

John 7:53–8:11 and 1 Corinthians 5 illustrate that while the ritual laws of the Old Testament are no longer observed, the moral laws of the Old Testament continue to be relevant to Christian behavior. Adultery was prohibited as the seventh commandment, and incest was forbidden in the case laws found in Leviticus 18 and 20. On the other hand, neither Jesus nor Paul appealed to the Old Testament penalty for these sins. Jesus saves the woman caught in adultery from stoning, which would have been her penalty during the time of the Old Testament, while Paul insists on what today would be called excommunication of the man sleeping with his mother. The difference in response to these breaches of the moral, as opposed to the ceremonial law, is explained by the fact that during the Old Testament time God's people were a nation-state that was called upon to be holy, while in the New Testament God's people are the church, a spiritual body, where physical punishments would be quite inappropriate.

In the Old Testament we saw that grace preceded law. However, contemporary teaching at the time of Jesus reversed that order and made a relationship with God dependent on obedience to the law. In Romans 3:9-30, Paul urgently teaches against this misunderstanding. The law reveals that everyone is a sinner. The law is not the answer to establishing a relationship with God; rather God in his grace enters into a relationship with us based on Christ's work. Christ was both the perfect keeper of the law as well as the one who bore the penalty for our sin. According to Matthew 22:34-40, though our relationship with God is based on grace, we express our gratitude and maintain that relationship by obeying God's will as it is expressed in the moral law. Jesus here reaffirms the general principles of the Ten Commandments by giving us two principles to live by: "Love the Lord your God with all your heart and with all your soul and with all your mind" (thus summarizing the first four commandments) and "Love your neighbor as yourself" (thus summarizing the last six commandments).

1. Describe Jesus' overall attitude toward the Old Testament law.

2. What was his attitude about the penalties of the Old Testament law?

◌ The Ancient Story and Our Story

If you completed the study in the previous section ("Anticipating the New Testament"), then you are well on your way to understanding how Christians should approach the Old Testament law. In the first place, Christians should know that we are saved not by keeping the law but by grace. Of course, that is the teaching of the Old Testament as well, but the temptation is often great to substitute our works for grace, and so the New Testament passionately teaches that God's grace, not our good deeds, leads to a vibrant relationship with God.

That said, the law still plays an important role in the Christian life as Jesus himself pointed out in Matthew 5:17-20. But, to use Jesus' words in that passage, there are some laws whose "purpose is achieved" (v. 18 NLT). These include laws that theologians today call "ceremonial," such as those concerning sacrifices, ritual purity, temple and priests (see more in study 9). The same is true of a group of laws known as civil laws, such as the law of kingship (Deuteronomy 17:14-20). After all, God's people are no longer a nation-state but are a spiritual entity. For this reason too the penalties of the Old Testament law (for example, the death penalty for being a witch) are no longer relevant. A third large category of laws, called moral laws, are still relevant. Most, but not all (the sabbath law is an exception, see again study 9), of the Ten Commandments are moral. So these laws still express God's will for our proper behavior, as do the case laws that are applications of the Ten Commandments, though often we have to apply them to our own situations, an example being Deuteronomy 22:8, which commands the building of a parapet (or fence) around a roof of a house. This law applies the principle of the sixth commandment not to murder to architecture because ancient Israelite houses used the roof as living space. But of course it would be ridiculous to say that houses, like most modern Western houses, have to build a parapet around their roof based on this law. Yet this law's principle reminds us that we should be mindful to build houses in ways that protect human life (for example, fences around swimming pools).

The bottom line is that the Old Testament law expresses God's will for our lives today. Though we have to approach it mindful of the differences between the time of the Old and New Testaments, it is still an important part of the Christian life.

LOOKING AHEAD

The law is an area in which the Christian often feels distance from the Old Testament. Another area of the Old Testament that Christians have a hard time relating to has to do with holy people (priests), places (sanctuaries) and actions (sacrifices). What is the meaning of these rituals, and how do Christians relate to them?

Going Deeper

Douma, Jochem. *The Ten Commandments: Manual for the Christian Life*. Phillipsburg, NJ: P & R, 1996.

Wright, Christopher J. H. *Old Testament Ethics for the People of God*. Downers Grove, IL: InterVarsity Press, 2004.

9 / Priests, Holy Place and Sacrifices

LOOKING AHEAD

MEMORY VERSE: Hebrews 9:11-14
BIBLE STUDY: Exodus 26; 29; 32; 1 Kings 7:13-51; Leviticus 1–3
READING: Coming into the Presence of the Lord

 Bible Study Guide

After reading Exodus 26; 29; 32; 1 Kings 7:13-51; Leviticus 1–3, spend some time reflecting on these passages with the following questions in mind before looking at the Reading.

1. What is a tabernacle?

2. Describe what the innermost curtain of the tabernacle looked like according to Exodus 26:1-6. What did this curtain symbolize?

3. What were the three outermost curtains of the tabernacle made of (Exodus 26:7-14)?

   What was their function?

4. What is the difference between the tabernacle and the temple?

Why do you think God commanded the tabernacle be replaced by the temple?

5. Why does the temple have so much garden imagery associated with it?

6. What is a priest in the Old Testament?

7. What did the Levites do to be set apart for priestly service to God according to Exodus 32?

Why do their actions on this occasion make them especially suitable for service as a priest?

8. What are the three different sacrifices mentioned in Leviticus 1–3?

9. Describe the ritual for a "burnt offering" (Leviticus 1).

What was its purpose?

10. Describe the ritual for a "grain offering" (Leviticus 2).

What was its purpose?

11. Describe the ritual for a "fellowship offering" (Leviticus 3).

What was its purpose?

⚇ Reading: Coming into the Presence of the Lord

Priests, holy places and sacrifices are strange to Christian experience. While some traditions refer to their ministers as priests, they do not function like Aaron and the Levites. Christians do not offer sacrifices as they did during the Old Testament period and there are no special places like the Old Testament tabernacle or temple where God made his special presence exclusively known. These people, places and actions were holy in the sense that they were "set apart" for special connection with the presence of God, and as we soon see, once Jesus came there was no longer any need for "set apart" people, places and actions.

HOLY PEOPLE: PRIESTS

In the Old Testament, priests were men who were consecrated for special service in the holy sanctuary (first the tabernacle and then the temple). Indeed, the ordination service described in Exodus 29 concludes by stating that both the tabernacle and the priests were consecrated (or set apart) together for special service to God (see especially vv. 44-46). Before describing the specific nature of their service, we will explore the choice of the tribe of Levites as priests. Why were Levites chosen?

The story actually begins back in Genesis 34, the rape of Dinah. While Jacob and his family lived in the vicinity of the Canaanite town of Shechem, Dinah had befriended some of the local girls. Once, when she went into town with them, she was violated by the prince of Shechem, a man named Shechem. Now Shechem wanted to marry her, so his father, Hamor, came to Jacob to ask for his permission to marry her. In ancient Israel it was customary for brothers to participate in their sister's marriage negotiations. Simeon and Levi were Dinah's full brothers (having not only the same father but the same mother—Leah). Jacob readily agreed to the marriage, but Simeon and Levi insisted that Shechem and all the men of the town be circumcised. While they claimed it was necessary because it was their custom, they had a more sinister intention in mind. Thus, after the Shechemites were circumcised and as a result in a weakened condition, Levi and Simeon attacked and killed them.

Their father, Jacob, was extremely angry with them because of their violence. They had ruined the family's reputation in the region, and the family would have to leave. Interestingly, the fact that the chapter ends with the brother's objection "Should he have treated our sister like a prostitute?" (Genesis 34:31) suggests that the narrator sides with the brothers. After all, it was not God's intention that the Israelites intermarry and settle down with the Canaanites.

Even so, at the end of his life, an angry Jacob curses Simeon and Levi because of their violence. He announces that they (by which he means their descendants, the later tribes of Simeon and Levi) would be condemned to be scattered in the land of Israel (Genesis 49:5-7). Sure enough, when we turn to the account of the distribution of the land to the various tribes of Israel, neither Simeon nor Levi receive an allotment of land, but are given towns within the boundaries of the other tribes of Israel (Joshua 19:1-9; 21).

The intention of Jacob's curse was for the Simeonites and Levites to lose their distinctive tribal identity as they were absorbed into the tribal territories of others. However, while this was the fate of the Simeonites, the Levites not only survived as a tribe, they actually became the most distinctive tribe of all. Why the difference?

At this point we come back to the story of the golden calf in Exodus 32. While Moses is on Mount Sinai receiving the Ten Commandments, the Israelites convinced Aaron to construct an idol in the form of a golden calf. When Moses came down from the mountain, he smashed the two stone tablets containing the commandments, symbolizing the breaking of the covenant between God and Israel. He then issued a call that those who were on the Lord's side come to him. The Levites responded, and Moses commanded them to go out among their fellow idol-worshiping Israelites and execute God's judgment. The Levites accordingly strapped on swords and killed three thousand calf worshipers.

Afterward, Moses announced, "You have been set apart to the LORD today, for you were against your own sons and brothers, and he has blessed you this day" (Exodus 32:29). The Levites had demonstrated

that they were willing and able to channel their propensity to violence in the service of God. The episode with the golden calf was something like a job interview that they passed with flying colors.

But what is it about their willingness to execute the calf worshipers that demonstrated their fitness for the priestly task? This question makes us explore more closely the nature and function of the priesthood in the Old Testament.

We begin by looking at Moses' blessing on the Levites at the end of his life in Deuteronomy 33:8-11:

> About Levi he said:
> "Your Thummim and Urim belong
>   to your faithful servant.
> You tested him at Massah;
>   you contended with him at the
>   waters of Meribah.
> He said of his father and mother,
>   'I have no regard for them.'
> He did not recognize his brothers
>   or acknowledge his own children,
> but he watched over your word
>   and guarded your covenant.
> He teaches your precepts to Jacob
>   and your law to Israel.
> He offers incense before you
>   and whole burnt offerings on
>   your altar.
> Bless all his skills, LORD,
>   and be pleased with the work of
>   his hands.
> Strike down those who rise against
>   him,
>   his foes till they rise no more."

We begin by noting the allusion back to Exodus 32, when the Levites went against their relatives in support of Moses against the apostasy of the golden calf. The key phrases that describe their motivation for their actions are "he [reference to the tribe of Levi] watched over your word" and "guarded your covenant." Here we have a concise description of the role of the priest: they protect the covenant relationship between God and his people Israel. It is not a stretch to say that they are the bodyguards of the holiness of God in relationship to Israel.

As bodyguards they take both preemptive and defensive actions. The former includes teaching the law of God so Israel knows the will of God and keeping them from violating their relationship with God. Related to this idea is their use of the Urim and Thummim. These are oracular devices (Exodus 28:30) that the high priest uses to determine the will of God (see example at Numbers 27:21). An example of a defensive action of the priests to preserve the sanctity of Israel's covenant relationship with God is offering sacrifices, particularly burnt offerings. These sacrifices are performed when there is a need to restore a relationship with God that has been broken by sin (see Leviticus 1).

HOLY PLACES: ALTARS,
TABERNACLE AND TEMPLE

Moving from "set apart" people (priests), we can now consider "set apart" places in the Old Testament. When the story begins in the Garden of Eden, there was no need for a holy place set apart for humans to meet with God. Adam and Eve could speak to God anywhere. However, the rebellion of Adam and Eve in Genesis 3 created a barrier between God and his creatures. Now they could only come into God's presence in specially designated locations. At first, when the people of God were an extended family, that place was marked by an altar. The Hebrew word for altar (*mizbeah*) is formed from a verb that means "to sacrifice" (*zabah*) and thus designates a place of sacrifice. The first altar mentioned in Scripture is the one built by Noah right after the flood waters receded and on which Noah offered God sacrifices (Genesis 8:20), but an altar is probably assumed as early as Genesis 4, when Cain and Abel gave their offerings to God. God's people built altars to mark holy ground where they could come into the presence of God.

A major change in the nature of the holy place occurred in the aftermath of the exodus (see Exodus 25–31; 35–40). God instructed Moses to build a tabernacle, which would include a sacrificial altar. God not only initiated the construction of the tabernacle, he also gave the plans (Exodus 25:9, 40; 26:30). God also supplied the precious metals and materials needed to build this ornate structure, since he moved the hearts of the Egyptian people to give them gifts on their way out of the land of their enslavement (Exodus 11:1-3). He even gave them the skills necessary for the work (Exodus 31:1-11).

The tabernacle was a tent that represented God's dwelling on earth. God's dwelling was a tent because his people were living in tents and not yet established in the land. This tent was the residence of the king and so was ornate, and like a king's tent it was located in the center of camp, surrounded by his bodyguards (the Levites) and then the rest of his people, who are described like an army on the march in Numbers 1–3.

The tabernacle was constructed in a manner that indicated that God lived there. The innermost part of the tabernacle was the most holy part of all. There the ark of the covenant, thought to be the footstool of God's throne, was placed. The cherubim figures whose wings covered the top of the ark faced down because not even these powerful spiritual beings could bear to look directly into the presence of God.

The innermost curtain of the tabernacle (Exodus 26:1-7), which served as the fabric roof of the tabernacle, was "finely twisted linen and blue, purple and scarlet yarn, with cherubim woven into them" (v. 1). In other words, the ceiling of the tabernacle would be a deep blue with cherubim figures, evoking a picture of heaven and symbolically indicating that the tabernacle was "heaven on earth." The three curtains placed on top of this precious innermost curtain (goat hair, ram skins dyed red, and durable leather [Exodus 26:7-14]) served as protection from the weather.

While more could be said about the furniture of the tabernacle, I will conclude with a look at the candlestick that provided illumination in the tabernacle (Exodus 25:31-40). Interestingly, the description of the construction of the candlestick (also known as the menorah) depicts it using the language of a flowering tree. The significance of this tree imagery is almost certainly to remind people of the Garden of Eden, a place where humanity met freely with God. Thus, it is appropriate to look at the imagery of the tabernacle as pointing to this place as heaven on earth and a return to Eden.

The tabernacle served as the holy place for many centuries, from the time of Moses to the time of Solomon. When Solomon became king, he quickly began the construction of the temple that ushered in a new way in which God made his presence known among his people (1 Kings 6–8).

The shape of God's sanctuary changes once again due to a change in the condition of the people of God. Before Israel was settled in the land, God made his presence known in a tent, but now that Israel was established in the land, a permanent residence or house was appropriate. David wanted to build the house for God, but he was the one who established Israel in the land by subduing the remaining internal enemies (see 2 Samuel 7:1-17). David was a warrior who shed much blood at God's command to rid the land of the remnants of their enemies; the temple would be built by Solomon, whose very name means "peace" (1 Chronicles 22:6-10).

Certain architectural features of the temple emphasize the theme of establishment. God instructed Solomon to build two pillars to stand in front of the temple (1 Kings 7:15-22). Pillars in and of themselves symbolize permanence, but they were also given names that pointed to this meaning. One was called Jakin ("he has established"), and the other was named Boaz ("by strength").

In addition, Solomon built a huge basin of water, holding about eleven thousand gallons, and named it the Sea (1 Kings 7:23-26). The significance of the name of this basin of water, Sea, goes back to ancient Near Eastern ideas that connect the sea with disorder, chaos, even evil. In defeating the internal enemies of Israel, God through David subdued the forces of chaos, and the bounded water of the Sea represents this great victory.

According to the description of the temple in 1 Kings 7, garden imagery is pervasive. Artistic representations of pomegranates and lilies adorned the capitals of the pillars (1 Kings 7:17-19). The sea was shaped like a gigantic water lily (v. 26). These representations of flora serve to remind the observer of the Garden of Eden, the place where God and his human creatures met without obstacle.

The temple was built by Solomon in the tenth century B.C., representing God's presence among his people. The building lasted for almost four hundred years, when it was destroyed by the Babylonians (2 Kings 25:8-17). God had abandoned the temple in anticipation of its destruction due to the sin of the people. After the exile the temple was rebuilt and completed about 515 B.C. This temple was the building that Jesus knew and visited during his ministry on earth.

HOLY ACTS: SACRIFICES

The priests were in charge of the sacrifices that took place in the holy place; they were an integral part of the sacred ritual of Israel. There are many different types of sacrifices described in the Old Testament, but the following three illustrate the three main purposes of sacrificial ritual before the coming of Christ. They are described in the first three chapters of Leviticus.

Leviticus 1 deals with the burnt offering (*'olah*), perhaps the most foundational sacrifice since it deals with atonement. The priests offered burnt offerings on behalf of Israelites who repented of their sins and sought to restore their broken relationship with God. The instructions for the burnt offering in Leviticus 1 states that the sacrifice can be of a bull, a sheep or goat, or even a bird. It is likely that the type of animal brought for the sacrifice depends on the economic status of the worshiper. Certainly, if a rich person brought a bird, that would reveal an unrepentant heart. The worshiper begins by laying hands on the head of the animal, thus ritually identifying with the animal. The animal stands in place of the sinner, and when the animal is completely burned it demonstrates that the sinner acknowledges that their sin deserved death.

The grain offering comes next in Leviticus 2. The Hebrew word translated "grain offering" (*minha*) literally means "gift" or "tribute," which is the purpose of this particular offering. The gift is grain, either cooked or uncooked. When the worshiper offers such an offering, the priest takes a representative portion, mixes it with oil and incense and burns that part on the altar as "an aroma pleasing to the LORD" (Leviticus 2:2). The rest is given to the priests for their use, but since the priests were dedicated to the service of God, this portion would also be considered a gift to God. Interestingly, the instructions for this sacrifice included the prohibition of adding either yeast or honey (Leviticus 2:11), but no explanation is given why. The best understanding of this prohibition is that yeast and honey (the Hebrew word specifically means fruit honey) ferment when burned, thus connecting it with decay and death. On the other hand, the instructions also insist that salt be added to this sacrifice. The salt represents "the covenant of your God" (Leviticus 2:13). Perhaps the fact that salt is not affected by fire and thus would have not burned up represents the eternal nature of the covenant that even survives the "fires of life."

Leviticus 3 then introduces a third type of offering that illustrates one more feature of the sacrificial system. The Hebrew word for this sacrifice (*shelamim*) is often translated in a way that makes explicit this feature: fellowship offering. Here only parts of the animal are burned in the fire; the rest is shared by the worshipers in a communal meal.

CONCLUSION

Priests, holy places and sacrifices were part of the core of Old Testament worship. However, they are not a part of the Christian experience. To understand why, we need to consider how the coming of Jesus affects the ritual observances of Israel.

Reading Study Guide

1. Why were the Levites chosen to be the priestly tribe?

2. Why is it appropriate to describe priests as bodyguards of God's holiness?

3. What is the connection between the Garden of Eden and the tabernacle and temple?

4. What explains the transition from altars to tabernacle to temple as the place where God's people worship him?

5. What features of the tabernacle make a worshiper think he or she is in heaven on earth?

6. What is it about the tabernacle or the temple that makes people think about the Garden of Eden?

7. What is the significance of the connection between tabernacle/temple and heaven and the Garden of Eden?

8. What is the significance of Israelite sacrifices?

9. Name the three major sacrifices as described in Leviticus 1–3 and their purposes.

10. Why was it important to add salt to the grain offering?

11. Why were yeast and honey prohibited?

➔ Anticipating the New Testament

Priests, holy places and sacrifices: perhaps no other area of Old Testament study feels as strange as the experience of Christians as the realm of Old Testament ritual ceremony. Why doesn't the church have holy places and priests or practice sacrifice today?

Priesthood. Melchizedek is one of the more mysterious figures of the Old Testament. When Abraham returned from defeating the four kings of the East, Melchizedek, described as king and priest of the city of Salem (the later Jerusalem), brought him bread and wine and blessed him. In return, Abram presented him with a tenth of the spoils of war (Genesis 14:17-20). It is surprising that Melchizedek, a Canaanite, worshiped the same God as Abram. We know little else about him.

Psalm 110 is a psalm of David, where David represents Yahweh as saying to him (the "my lord" of v. 1), "You are a priest forever, in the order of Melchizedek" (v. 4). While the Israelite Levitical tradition separated the idea of king and priest, Melchizedek united the two roles. Jesus is both priest and king, as well as a descendant of David, and this suggested to the author of Hebrews that Jesus was a superior priest to Aaron and the Levitical line and encouraged him to make a connection with Melchizedek (Hebrews 7). To say that Jesus was a priest in the line of Melchizedek is a way of saying he is a vastly superior priest to Aaron.

Holy places. During the Old Testament period, there were special holy places, first marked by simple altars, then the tabernacle, and finally the temple. Jesus is the very presence of God, and when he departed this earth, he sent the Holy Spirit, who dwells in us. No longer are special holy places needed. (For more on this see Matthew 27:51-53; Mark 13:1-2; 14:57-59; John 1:14; 4:21-24.)

Sacrifices. The chief function of a sacrifice was atonement. In an atonement sacrifice the animal stood in place of the sinner and suffered the fate that the sinner deserved, death. According to the New Testament, though, it "is impossible for the blood of bulls and goats to take away sins" (Hebrews 10:4). Their only significance is that they anticipated the sacrifice that would really matter, namely Jesus, God's son, who died on the cross for our benefit. By this sacrifice, "he has made perfect forever those who are being made holy" (Hebrews 10:14). (For more on Old Testament sacrificial system and Jesus' sacrifice read Hebrews 9:11–10:18.)

1. In what way does Jesus relate to Old Testament priests?

2. Why does Jesus' coming render a sanctuary like the temple unnecessary?

3. Why don't Christians offer sacrifices today?

◯ The Ancient Story and Our Story

Priests, holy places and sacrifices are all part of the ceremonial worship of ancient Israel. Perhaps there is no other area where there is more distance between Old Testament and New Testament practice. Since Jesus is the fulfillment of the priesthood, the holy place and sacrifices, we no longer anoint priests, go to holy places or offer sacrifices.

However, the New Testament speaks of priests, holy places and sacrifices in a way that bears on our self-understanding as well as our behavior.

While a number of New Testament passages speak to this idea, Peter puts all three together when he says that as Christians we "are being built into a spiritual house to be a holy priesthood, offering spiritual sacrifices acceptable to God through Jesus Christ" (1 Peter 2:5).

An alternate translation of "spiritual house" is "temple of the Spirit." In other words, just as the presence of God filled the Old Testament temple, so the Holy Spirit fills us, rendering us holy, or set apart, which has implications for how we live. As a temple of God, we should not engage in sinful activities. Here Paul says, "What agreement is there between the temple of God and idols? For we are the temple of the living God" (2 Corinthians 6:16). Elsewhere, he warns against sexual immorality because "your bodies are temples of the Holy Spirit" (1 Corinthians 6:19).

We are also priests, furthering our responsibility to be holy. We represent God in the world. We are guardians of God's holiness. We also offer sacrifices, not of animals but spiritual sacrifices. Paul urges us, "in view of God's mercy, to offer your bodies as a living sacrifice, holy and pleasing to God" (Romans 12:1).

LOOKING AHEAD

After our study of Old Testament rituals—priests, holy places and sacrifices—we return to the history of redemption. God initiated the building of the tabernacles, anointed the first priests and gave instructions concerning the offering of sacrifices while in the wilderness, and it is to the wilderness that we turn again in study 10.

Going Deeper

Longman, Tremper, III. *Immanuel in Our Place*. Phillipsburg, NJ: P & R, 2001.

10 / Conquest

LOOKING AHEAD

MEMORY VERSE: Psalm 136:17-22
BIBLE STUDY: Deuteronomy 20; Joshua 1–12; 13:1-7; 15; 24
READING: God Gives His People the Land

 **Bible Study Guide**

After reading Deuteronomy 20; Joshua 1–12; 13:1-7; 15; 24, spend some time reflecting on these passages with the following questions in mind before looking at the Reading. (For maximum benefit read the entire book of Joshua.)

1. What message does God deliver to Joshua in Joshua 1?

2. Using Rahab as an example, what happens to Canaanites who support and help the Israelites?

3. What happens to the waters of the Jordan River (Joshua 3–4), when Joshua and the Israelites cross over to the Promised Land?

   What earlier event does this remind you of?

4. Why did the Israelites circumcise all their men and observe Passover after crossing the Jordan (Joshua 5:2-12)?

5. Jericho is the most powerful of the Canaanite city-states at the time. Describe in your own words the battle of Jericho (Joshua 6).

6. Ai is among the weakest city-states at the time. The name Ai even means "dump." Why then did Israel lose the first battle of Ai and win the second (Joshua 7–8)?

7. What did Joshua do wrong in his handling of the emissaries of the Gibeonites (Joshua 9)?

8. How did Joshua and the Israelites defeat the armies of southern (Joshua 10) and northern (Joshua 11) Canaan?

9. Read Joshua 13:1-7. Are you surprised that "very large areas of land" are still controlled by the Canaanites even after the conquest?

10. Read Joshua 15. Here the boundaries for the tribe of Judah are given. What is the significance for the original audience that such detailed descriptions of tribal allotments are given?

11. Why does Joshua lead Israel in a renewal of their covenantal commitment to the Lord at the end of his life (Joshua 24)?

Reading: God Gives His People the Land

The Torah ended with the Israelites encamped on the plains of Moab, just across the Jordan River from the mighty Canaanite city of Jericho. Moses, their great leader, had led them through the wilderness for the past forty years, but at the end of the book of Deuteronomy, he ascended Mount Nebo, where he would die. Due to Moses' rebellion (Numbers 20:1-13), God did not permit him to accompany the Israelites into the land. Indeed, none of the adult generation of Israel that had left Egypt would be permitted into the land (see study 7).

As the book of Joshua opens, Joshua has replaced Moses as the leader of the people. He would lead them across the Jordan River and guide them in battle against the Canaanites. Such a task was formidable, and the book begins with God assuring Joshua that he would be with him as he was with Moses (Joshua 1:5). When God promised to be "with" someone, that was shorthand for saying that he was in covenant with them and would support them with his power and wisdom. In response, Joshua needed to be "strong and very courageous" (vv. 6-7). In addition, he must obey the law that God had given Israel (vv. 7-8).

Joshua thus began the preparations necessary for entry into the land, which includes battle against the Canaanites. Before the invasion Joshua sent spies into the city of Jericho. Jericho was the most powerful and dangerous of the Canaanite city-states. The Canaanites were not a united nation but rather a number of city-states that were under the leadership of Egypt. We know from extrabiblical texts (Amarna tablets) that these city-states were under the treaty protectorate of Egypt, but we also know that Egypt at this time was not in a position to be much help to them.

Before crossing the Jordan, Joshua ordered spies to infiltrate the city of Jericho (Joshua 2), and when they do, they go to a place where strangers would not be immediately noticed, the inn of a prostitute named Rahab. Eventually, the king of Jericho suspected that spies had gone to the inn, but Rahab covered up their presence in return for the promise that the Israelites would not harm her or her family. This story illustrates that it was possible for Canaanites like Rahab to choose to be on Israel's side and avoid the fate that awaited those who resisted them.

Before the Israelites cross the Jordan River into the Promised Land, Joshua orders that they perform a mass ritual of circumcision (Joshua 5:2-12). Apparently, those who were born in the wilderness period were not circumcised, though the reason why is not clear. What is clear is that Joshua understands that God feels that it is important that the men are circumcised before they enter the land. We remember from the strange story in Exodus 4:24-25 that God takes circumcision, which is after all the sign of the Abrahamic covenant (Genesis 17), very seriously. The Abrahamic covenant was the one in which God promised the patriarch that his descendants would become a "great nation" (Genesis 12:2), and land is an important part of that promise. In addition, the people observed Passover in preparation for the entry into the land. After all, God would be fighting for them as a warrior against their superior enemies, the Canaanites, and so his people would need to be spiritually prepared to be in his presence.

When they do cross the Jordan, a marvelous event takes place. The waters of the Jordan stop flowing so the people of Israel can cross over on dry ground. This act of God was not just for the purpose of keeping them dry. The dry Jordan would remind the second generation of the story of the crossing of the Reed Sea, which they would have heard from their parents. God was telling the Israelites that he, the God who had defeated the powerful Egyptians, would be with them as they faced the powerful Canaanites in battle.

The first three battles impart three different lessons to Israel. The first battle is against Jericho, which I have already commented is the most powerful city-state in Canaan. Jericho was the oldest city in the region, renowned for its massive walls.

Before the battle, Joshua encounters Yahweh, his God, looking like a warrior, who gives him instructions for the battle (Joshua 5:13-15). Israel is not to attack the city in a conventional way, but to march around the city for six days. On the sev-

enth and final day the Israelites would blow trumpets (signaling the arrival of God the warrior) and the walls would fall down, allowing the Israelite soldiers to enter the city. Everything happened as God said it would, and this seemingly impregnable city fell easily to Israel.

The story of Jericho contrasts dramatically with the account of the second battle against the city of Ai. While Jericho was the most formidable city in Canaan, Ai was insignificant. As a matter of fact, the name "Ai" means "dump" or "ruin." Joshua is so unimpressed that he sends only a small number of troops. However, while Israel easily defeated the mighty Jericho, they were soundly defeated by the lowly Ai. Why? Because one person, Achan, disobeyed God's command that no one should benefit from the plunder of defeated enemies. Once Achan was found out and executed, Israel could defeat Ai.

Thus, the lesson of the first two battle accounts is clear. If Israel listens and obeys Yahweh, they will be victorious in battle, even against the mightiest of their enemies. However, if they are disobedient, even their weakest opponent will resist and defeat them.

The third major episode of the conquest illustrates yet one more important lesson. After Ai, the Israelites returned to their war camp in the city of Gilgal. One day a group of tired men, riding weary horses and carrying stale food showed up at the camp. These men represented themselves as ambassadors of a people far away who wanted to enter into a treaty relationship with Israel. Deuteronomy 20:10-20 provides background to this story:

> When you march up to attack a city, make its people an offer of peace. If they accept and open their gates, all the people in it shall be subject to forced labor and shall work for you. If they refuse to make peace and they engage you in battle, lay siege to that city. When the LORD your God delivers it into your hand, put to the sword all the men in it. As for the women, the children, the livestock and everything else in the city, you may take these as plunder for yourselves. And you may use the plunder the LORD your God gives you from your enemies. This is how you are to treat all the cities that are at a distance from you and do not belong to the nations nearby.
>
> However, in the cities of the nations the LORD your God is giving you as an inheritance, do not leave alive anything that breathes. Completely destroy them—the Hittites, Amorites, Canaanites, Perizzites, Hivites and Jebusites—as the LORD your God has commanded you. Otherwise, they will teach you to follow all the detestable things they do in worshiping their gods, and you will sin against the LORD your God.

Thinking that the Gibeonites were outside the land, Joshua entered into a treaty with them only to discover that they were really from just down the road within the land! The narrator of Joshua points out that Joshua did not inquire of Yahweh (Joshua 9:14) as he should have done. Thus, Israel learns a third lesson the hard way. It is crucial to know God's will. Later in Israel's history, the presence of Gibeon will become a major problem.

Jericho, Ai and Gibeon are the three longest episodes in the account of the conquest due to the book's desire to emphasize these important theological and moral lessons to later Israel. Obedience brings victory, while a failure to know God's will or, even worse, disobedience results in defeat. Even so, at the end of these first three episodes, the Israelites now control the central part of the Promised Land, cutting off the kings of the north from the kings of the south.

The next phase of the battle is initiated by Canaanites, not the Israelites. As mentioned already, the Amarna tablets indicate to us that the Canaanites were not tightly united with each other. The various cities were independent, and each was ruled by a different king. The tablets further indicate that there was considerable rivalry between these kings. The book of Joshua, though, informs us that once Joshua and the Israelites invaded the land and defeated Jericho and Ai and incorporated Gibeon, the kings quickly formed an alliance. The north and the south, though, were divided by the Israelites, who held the middle. Thus, the remaining Canaanites formed two blocks. The first to be described in the book (Joshua 10) were the kings of the south. They united into a single alliance and attacked the Gibeonites, presumably for allying themselves with Israel. Joshua and the Israelites were in their war camp in Gilgal when they received news of this attack. Since they were now in a treaty relationship with the Gibeonites, they were duty bound to attack the southern coalition. As it turned out, the southern Canaanites had done them a favor by leaving their walled cities and taking to the open battlefield. Thus rather than needing to attack city after city and laying what might have turned out to be long sieges, the Israelites could defeat the armies of southern Canaan in a single battle, and they did so, with the Lord's help. The Lord's help came in two forms. First he rained hailstones down on the heads of the Canaanite armies. These hailstones killed more Canaanites than did the Israelites' weapons. God also made his presence known as warrior in this battle by "stopping" the sun and the moon in the sky. What God exactly did here has been the subject of endless speculation and debate. The Hebrew is admittedly not all that clear. Did the heavenly bodies actually suspend motion? Is this a reference to an eclipse or some refraction of the sun's light? Unfortunately, we cannot say with certainty. However, what we can say with great confidence is that God caused the day to prolong in a marvelous way so Israel could complete their victory over the Canaanites who had set out to defeat them.

After hearing about the defeat of the southern coalition of the Canaanite kings, the story now turns to the northern kings, who likewise join together to attack the Israelites. They too take to the open battlefield rather than staying behind their cities' defensive walls. And once again the Israelites decisively defeat the armies of these Canaanite kings with God's help (Joshua 11:6).

Joshua 12 is a celebrative summary statement listing the kings of Canaan whom Joshua and Israel had defeated with God's power. It should be pointed out, particularly in the light of the fact that archaeological research has not shown extensive damage to these cities at this time, that what the Bible describes for the most part is the defeat of kings in the open battlefield, not the actual subjugation of the cities themselves. While some cities and parts of the Promised Land are taken and occupied by Israel, much land remains under weakened Canaanite control. Nonetheless, Joshua 1–12 emphasizes the victories over the Canaanites because it is celebrating the beginning of the fulfillment of God's promise to Abraham that his descendants would become a great nation, and of course that promise includes the idea that they would have a land that was their own.

The second half of the book of Joshua majors in describing the distribution of land to the various tribes of Israel (Joshua 13–21). Most modern readers find this part of the book of Joshua boring. After all, the boundaries of the tribes are delineated by long lists of towns and villages, many having names that are difficult to pronounce. Most readers give up and just skip to a more interesting section of Scripture. In neglecting this portion of Scripture, we miss its important theological significance.

In the first place we should note that the land was distributed according to God's intentions for each of the tribes. There was no planning committee that sat around for days figuring out which tribe would go where. God made his will known through the casting of lots (Joshua 14:1-6). The high priest, in this case Eleazar, had possession of the sacred lots, known elsewhere as the Urim and Thummim (Exodus 28:29-30). We do not know for certain how they function, but they were "thrown," making us think they were dice-like objects. How they were used on this occasion is not precisely known, but it does indicate that the tribes received their allotments from God.

Let's remember that God gave Abraham a promise that his descendants would become a "great nation" (Genesis 12:2). This promise, given many centuries before, anticipates not only that he would have a great many descendants but that they would eventually receive the Promised Land of Canaan (Genesis 15:1-20). That moment had come at long last! The long-awaited fulfillment of the promise had arrived. Placing ourselves in the footsteps of this generation of Israelites, we can imagine their excitement as the promise of the land was becoming concrete. After their lengthy period of slavery and wandering, every village name would have thrilled them to the bone.

That said, the promise of land was not completely fulfilled. As mentioned earlier, much land remained yet to be conquered in the future. Enough had been taken to allow the Israelites to formally distribute the land to the tribes, but now the tribes had to continue to push the Canaanites out of the land. The promise was already, but not yet completely, realized. Shortly, we will see how our own relationship to the promises of God is similar to that of the Israelites at this time.

Before leaving the account of the distribution of the land to the tribes, we should pay close attention to the way two of the tribes are treated. Neither the Simeonites nor the Levites received a tribal allotment. Rather, Simeon's descendants were given towns within the boundaries of the tribe of Judah (Joshua 19). The Levites were given a number of towns scattered throughout the other tribes of Israel (Joshua 21). The reason for this different treatment arises from Genesis 49:5-7, when Simeon and Levi's father cursed them for their violent actions in the city of Shechem. While the author of the Genesis 34 account seems to side with the son's actions since Jacob's complaint was that they could not intermarry and settle down with the Canaanites, nonetheless Jacob's curse takes effect here in the aftermath of the conquest. The intention of the curse is that these two tribes would eventually lose their distinctive identities and be absorbed into the other tribes. As we noted in study 9, though, the Levites' godly action on the occasion of the false worship of the golden calf won them status as a priestly tribe. Far from losing their distinctive identity, the Levites become the most distinctive tribe of all. Their story is an example of bringing a blessing out of a curse.

The conquest and settlement narrative comes to an end in the same way that the Torah, or Books of Moses, comes to an end—with a renewal of the covenant. Like the end of Deuteronomy, Israel's great leader, then Moses, now Joshua, is about to die. At this moment of transition, Israel is in a vulnerable spiritual position. Will they continue to be faithful to God, or will they rebel and sin? Joshua thus reminds them of their fundamental obligation to love and obey God. He first recounts to them the long history of their relationship with God, pointing out how good he has been to them (Joshua 24:2-13). On that basis he calls on them to "fear the LORD and serve him with all faithfulness. Throw away the gods your ancestors worshiped" (v. 14). He warns them that if they don't, then God who "is a jealous God . . . will turn and bring disaster on you and make an end of you, after he has been good to you" (vv. 19-20). The book ends with the people agreeing to follow the Lord; then comes an account of Joshua's death. We have to turn to the next book, Judges, to find out if the people follow through on their promise to follow God. Unfortunately, the answer is nothing short of tragic.

Reading Study Guide

1. Look again at the battles of Jericho and Ai and the incident at Gibeon (Joshua 6–9). What led to success and what led to failure?

   Is there a lesson for modern readers here?

2. What do we learn from the Amarna tablets about Canaan at the time of Joshua?

3. Why did Israel need to be spiritually prepared by circumcising the men and observing Passover before going into the Promised Land to fight the Canaanites?

4. Where in Joshua 1–12 do you see God acting like a warrior?

5. God appears as a warrior to fight on behalf of Israel in various battles. How do you react to the idea that God is a warrior who kills Canaanites?

6. What advantage came to the Israelites when kings in the south and kings in the north banded together into coalitions in order to fight Israel on the open battlefield?

7. Modern archaeologists have found little evidence of the destruction of Canaanite cities mentioned in Joshua 1–12. Does this create a problem? Why or why not?

8. What is the theological significance of the chapters devoted to the distribution of the land to the tribes (Joshua 13–23)?

   Is there any message here for modern readers?

9. What is distinctive and significant about the way Simeon and Levi's descendants were treated during the distribution of the tribes?

10. What was Joshua trying to accomplish at the end of his life when he led the people in a renewal of the covenant in Joshua 24?

Anticipating the New Testament

God appears as a warrior in the pages of the book of Joshua as Israel conquers the Canaanites and begins to settle in the Promised Land. Here and elsewhere we read about God who fights and wins battles against Israel's flesh-and-blood enemies. However, the Old Testament also records times when God comes against Israel as a warrior.

Lamentations is Israel's response to the destruction of Jerusalem at the hands of the Babylonians (see study 17). In Lamentations 2 God is described not as a warrior who fights on behalf of his people but as one who comes as an enemy against them because of their sins.

However, the Old Testament does not end with the story of the destruction of Israel but with a note of hope. While God's people continue to live under the domination of foreign powers, God uses the prophets of the time to tell them that he will come as a warrior in the future in order to free them from their oppression (e.g., Zechariah 14). Zechariah, who lives toward the end of the Old Testament time period, after the restoration of Judah from their exile in Babylon, is an example of one whom God uses to bring this message to his people.

While many people likely expected a Messiah who would wage war against the oppressive Romans, Jesus came to fight a far more important battle—one that was waged against the spiritual "powers and authorities" that hold people captive (Ephesians 6:10-20). Jesus is the warrior who won this battle by dying on the cross and through his resurrection (Colossians 2:13-15).

And Jesus will come again as a warrior, and this time he will win the final victory over all evil, both human and spiritual (Revelation 19:11-21).

1. How do the appearances of God in the Old Testament anticipate the coming of Jesus as a warrior?

2. Ephesians 6:10-20 describes the Christian's war as "against the rulers, against the authorities, against the powers of this dark world and against the spiritual forces of evil in the heavenly realms." According to Paul, what weapons do we use against such an enemy?

○ The Ancient Story and Our Story

The picture of God as a warrior in the book of Joshua (and elsewhere in the Old Testament) often disturbs modern readers, particularly since God's command to Joshua to battle Canaanites seems at odds with Jesus' well-known teaching to "turn the other cheek" (Matthew 5:39) and "love your enemies" (Matthew 5:44).

A careful consideration of the Bible as a whole demonstrates that these pictures of God are not opposites but are part of God's plan to defeat sin and evil in a fallen world. Knowing this plan as it is revealed in the Bible helps us understand our place in relationship to the Israelites in the book of Joshua.

In the Old Testament, God fought for Israel, except for those occasions when they disobeyed him. In those cases, like at the time of the Babylonian destruction of Jerusalem and exile, God fought against Israel to judge them for their sins. Even so, God did not abandon his people. He restored them to the land and directed his postexilic prophets, Zechariah and others, to tell his people that he would come again as a warrior. After all, though restored to the land, they still suffered under the oppression of the Persians and eventually the Greeks and the Romans. During the time period between the Old and New Testaments, the expectation of a warring Messiah (anointed king) sent by God grew.

The New Testament informs us that Jesus is that Messiah, but rather than leading his people in a physical battle against the Romans, he heightens and intensifies the battle so that now it is directed toward the spiritual powers and authorities. And these enemies are not defeated by swords and spears (notice Jesus' command to Peter to "put your sword back in its place" [Matthew 26:52]), but by his death, resurrection and ascension (see Ephesians 4:7-10; Colossians 2:13-15).

The New Testament also looks to the future in passages like Revelation 19:11-21, when Jesus will return. When he does, he will come as a warrior to rescue his people and put an end to all evil—both flesh-and-blood as well as spiritual.

We live in the period between the first and second coming of Christ. We look back on the battles of Joshua and other Old Testament saints and look forward to the coming of Christ. We live in a time of spiritual warfare. A passage like Ephesians 6:10-20 describes the battle we wage against "evil rulers and authorities of the unseen world, against mighty powers in this dark world, and against evil spirits in the heavenly places" (Ephesians 6:12 NLT). Paul here explains that we do not do it alone but with God's help. So we are to "put on all of God's armor so that you will be able to stand firm against all strategies of the devil" (Ephesians 6:11 NLT). Thus, as we encounter the chaos and evil of the world, we are to remember that we don't fight alone but in God's strength, knowing that the victory will ultimately be his.

LOOKING AHEAD

Joshua recounts the conquest and the settlement of the land of Canaan. While Israel was far from fully occupying the land of promise, they were now firmly entrenched there. The book ends with the Israelites reaffirming their commitment to stay loyal to God in the future after the death of their great leader Joshua.

As we turn to the book of Judges, we will see just how well God's people lived up to their commitment. What we discover will be disturbing and disappointing.

Going Deeper

Hubbard, Robert L., Jr. *Joshua*. NIV Application Commentary. Grand Rapids: Zondervan, 2009.

Longman, Tremper, III, and Daniel G. Reid. *God Is a Warrior*. Grand Rapids: Zondervan, 1995.

11 / Judges

LOOKING AHEAD

MEMORY VERSE: Judges 21:25
BIBLE STUDY: Judges 1:1–3:6; 3:12-30; 13–16; 17–18; Ruth
READING: Spiritual Confusion, Moral Depravity, Political Fragmentation

 ## Bible Study Guide

After reading Judges 1:1–3:6; 3:12-30; 13–16; 17–18 and Ruth, spend some time reflecting on these passages with the following questions in mind before looking at the Reading. (For maximum benefit read the books of Judges and Ruth in their entirety.)

1. Judges 1 describes events after the death of Joshua. What do we learn about the status of Israel's occupation of the land in relationship to the Canaanites?

2. Judges 2:10-19 gives a general overview of what might be called the cycle of the book of Judges. Beginning with the sin of the people and ending with the people sinning again, list all the different steps of this cycle.

3. Read the story of Ehud (Judges 3:12-30) and point out the steps of the cycle of Judges (see question 2) present in this story.

4. Would you consider Ehud a good man or a bad one? For what reason?

5. Read the story of Micah and the Levite (Judges 17–18). Are there any good characters in this story?

6. Explain how the story of Micah's family turns into a story of a troubled nation.

7. Contrast the picture of Israel in the book of Judges with what we learn about Israel from the book of Ruth.

Reading: Spiritual Confusion, Moral Depravity, Political Fragmentation

The book of Joshua ends with an account of the death and burial of Joshua, Israel's leader during the perilous time of the Conquest. After the distribution of the land to the various tribes, Joshua led them in a ritual that reaffirmed the covenant that was central to their relationship with God. They had agreed to follow and obey God in the future. The book of Judges paints a picture of the next generations "after the death of Joshua" (Judges 1:1), and that picture is not pretty. The book of Judges gives us stories about the time period after the death of Joshua and before the rise of the monarchy, which informs the reader that this was a time of moral depravity, political fragmentation and spiritual darkness.

The book of Judges can be divided into three major parts. After a brief introduction (Judges 1:1–2:5), the long middle section describes the activity of the "judges," whose role gives the book its name. With stories about Othniel, Ehud, Shamgar, Deborah, Gideon, Jephthah, Samson and others, this part of the book is the best known among modern readers. Most of these stories roughly share the same structure (the "cycle of judges"). This structure is announced in the opening episode of this section (Judges 2:1–3:6). After a period of peace, the people would sin, here identified as the sin of idolatry. As a consequence God would send a foreign nation to oppress and occupy a part of the land. After the people repented (crying out to God), God would raise up a judge, who then delivered them from their enemies and led them to another period of peace. This peace was short-lived, because soon enough the people would sin again and the cycle would begin again. A close reading shows that the people get worse and worse as time goes on, so it is not so much that they are going in a dark circle but rather they are in a death spiral. The conclusion of the book (Judges 17–21) presents two further stories set in this troubled time period. As we will see, they both start with the account of a troubled family, whose story escalates to a troubled nation.

The preface makes clear what the second half of Joshua describes, namely, that the wars of Joshua may have broken the back of the Canaanites, but they did not completely subdue them. Much land remains to be taken under Israelite control. For instance, Jerusalem, the future capital of a united Israel, is still under Canaanite control. Judges 1 describes how the tribe of Judah takes Jerusalem and burns it with fire. However, we know from later Scripture that that important Canaanite city does not come permanently into Israelite control until the time of David (2 Samuel 5:6-16). In Judges 2:3 God himself informs the Israelites why they were not successful in completely removing the Canaanites from the land. Israel has disobeyed God and thus, "I will not drive them out before you; they will become traps for you, and their gods will become snares to you."

The second and longest part of Joshua describes the rise of the judges. For reasons not explained in the Bible, Joshua, who had replaced Moses as leader of the tribes, is not replaced by a single individual. Left to their own devices the Israelites sin against God. Specifically, they wander after other gods, with the result that God turns them over to an oppressor. It is only when they cry out to God for help, thus showing their utter dependence on God, that God sends a judge to save them, who initiates a new period of peace.

To illustrate the pattern, earlier described as part of a death spiral, we will explore the narrative concerning Ehud, a relatively unknown judge.

But first we need to look a bit closer at the question of the function of these judges. Indeed, the term *judge* is slightly misleading. When we think of a judge, we think of the courtroom and a person who presides over a trial to determine the innocence or guilt of a defendant. While some judges, notably Deborah, function in this way (Judges 4:5), most do not. One cannot imagine Samson in a courtroom, for instance. The Hebrew word translated "judge" is best understood to point not to a judicial function but rather a military one. A judge is a "deliverer" or "rescuer." God raises up these individuals in order to save the Israelites from their enemies.

In addition, while the narrative, when read superficially, gives the sense that these judges acted sequentially and on behalf of the whole nation, a closer reading reveals that they sometimes overlapped with each other and were influential in a certain region of Israel. Simple mathematics indicates this. The book of Judges names the length of time for periods of peace and periods of oppression. If all of these dates are added up, they far exceed the time period between the Conquest and the rise of the monarchy. In addition, we even get statements that place two judges at the same time period. For instance, in the preface to the story of Jephthah the narrator informs the reader that, due to the false worship of the Israelites, "he [God] became angry with them. He sold them into the hands of the Philistines and the Ammonites, who that year shattered and crushed them" (Judges 10:7-8). The story then goes on to talk about how God used Jephthah to rid Israel of the Ammonites in the northeast of Israel (Judges 10:6–12:7) and then how he used Samson to crush the Philistine oppression in the southwest (Judges 13–16).

Ehud is a good short example of a judge in Israel (Judges 3:12-30). Ehud is one of the early judges, and the early judges (Othniel, Ehud, Deborah) are not themselves deeply tainted figures as we will see the later judges are. That said, the story of Ehud is a dark one, as we see when we read the passage carefully.

The story begins with the formula that indicates that Israel rebelled against God. Though the statement is somewhat vague here ("Israel did evil in the eyes of the LORD"), the preface to the second part of the book makes it clear that worship of false gods is what brings on God's anger (see Judges 2:11-13).

As a result, God allows an oppressor to take over part of the land of Israel. In this case Eglon, the king of Moab, takes over the city of Jericho and its surrounding area. Interestingly, in the light of the later events in the story, the name Eglon means "fat calf." Eventually, after eighteen years of oppression, the Israelites repent ("cried out to the LORD" [Judges 3:15]), and God raised up a judge whose name was Ehud.

Ehud must have been a leader of the Benjamite tribe, because he was charged with delivering the tribute to the king of Moab, who is described as very fat. Since Hebrew narrative rarely gives physical descriptions of its characters, we can already assume that Eglon's girth will play a role in the story. The same is true for Ehud's left-handedness. In the first place, the fact that he is a left-handed Benjamite would have elicited chuckles, since Benjamite means "son of the right hand." But more seriously the fact that he was left-handed explains how he got beyond security later, since being left-handed was not only rare but avoided since it was considered abnormal. The text points out that Ehud, as opposed to everyone else, wore his sword on his right thigh, a place the palace security would not have checked.

Ehud delivered the tribute, but then, on his return trip, when he passed by the "stone images near Gilgal," he turned back to Jericho. Perhaps it was the images that kindled his righteous anger; the text does not explicitly state this, though it likely implies it. Whatever motivated him to return, when he enters the court, he tells Eglon that he has a "secret message" (Judges 3:19) for him. Eglon then dismisses all of his attendants, including his bodyguard to hear this "secret message." In the next scene Eglon and Ehud are alone in an "upper room" of the palace, a place many believe is a bathroom. After all, later in the story his attendants do not immediately go into this upper room because they fear he might be "relieving himself" (v. 24). Indeed, the rare Hebrew word that is translated "porch" in verse 23 is thought by many to be a latrine pipe (see NLT).

Why would Eglon dismiss his bodyguards and go to a private room, perhaps the bathroom, with an emissary of the enemy? To ask the question is to answer it. He heard "secret message" as a romantic overture. But while he expected one type of penetration, Ehud gave him another. Revealing that his secret message came from God, Ehud plunged his sword into Eglon's body. Eglon was so fat that the sword was completely absorbed by his body, and he emptied his bowls. Of course, the smell is what made the attendants think that the king might be relieving himself, giving Ehud ample time to escape.

Eglon was dead. The Moabites were in disarray and easily removed from Israel. Ehud, God's appointed agent of deliverance, thus expelled the Moabites and established a period of peace.

The story of the judges showed how bad times were, but the appendix adds two stories that rival the account of the judges for revealing how wicked people were during this time. These two stories have a different structure than the earlier part of the book, though these two share a structure between them. These stories add to the impression of spiritual confusion, moral darkness and political fragmentation. Both narratives begin as the story of a dysfunctional family and move to the account of a dysfunctional nation.

The first story is found in Judges 17–18 and begins with an introduction to the main character Micah and his relationship with his mother. Micah opens by confessing to his mother that he was the culprit who stole eleven hundred shekels of silver from her (Judges 17:2). But what looks like a story of confession and repentance becomes the occasion for trouble. Micah's mother displays her confusion when she celebrates the restoration of her relationship with her son and the recovery of the money by inexplicably proclaiming, "I solemnly consecrate my silver to the LORD for my son to make an image overlaid with silver" (v. 3). Anyone who knows the Ten Commandments knows that one should not build an image, even one dedicated to God (see Exodus 20:4-6).

Micah takes this image and constructs a little shrine. His own son functioned as a priest, that is, until a Levite wandered by. Levites, of course, were the tribe set aside for special service to the Lord and his holy place (see study 9). They should be destroying, not supporting, private shrines like Micah's. However, this Levite readily takes the job as Micah's priest. Micah then asserts, "Now I know that the LORD will be good to me, since this Levite has become my priest" (v. 13). One marvels at his utter spiritual confusion!

The next chapter takes the story to a national level as some men from the tribe of Dan pass through the area and notice Micah's shrine. These men are a vanguard of the Danites looking for a new place for their tribe to settle. Just the mere fact that they are considering relocation is a sign of moral, spiritual and political trouble. After all, they had been assigned their present place by God himself right after the conquest (Joshua 19:40-48), but apparently they were unsatisfied with God's gift. They ask the Levite serving Micah's shrine to ask God whether their trip would be successful. The Levite, whom we already know is not serving God correctly, gives them his blessing (vv. 5-6). After they find new land to the far north, they return to get the rest of the fighting men of Dan. As this larger group came back through the region where Micah lived, they took Micah's idol and convinced his Levite to go with them. Micah unsuccessfully tried to stop them, so they continued up and took the new land and settled there (vv. 14-25). A later Israelite reader of this story would understand that this story provides precedent for the later building of a golden calf shrine in the city of Dan that was the occasion of disobedience on the part of the northern kingdom of Israel (1 Kings 12:25-33; see study 15).

The second story (Judges 19–21), in the appendix of Judges, also begins with a family tragedy when a Levite's concubine ran away from her husband to return home to Bethlehem. After a period of time, the Levite, who lived in the hill country of Ephraim, went down to retrieve her. When he arrived, the concubine's father did everything he possibly could to delay their return. Finally, the Levite insisted on leaving with his concubine. However, they did not depart until the middle of the day, so they could not make the trip home in a single day. While refusing to spend the night in the pagan city of Jebus (the future Jerusalem), they continue on to the city of Gibeah, just to the north.

Though an Israelite town, they receive no immediate hospitality until an out-of-towner from the tribe of Ephraim brings them into his home and warns them about spending time in public places. His reasons come clear when some men from the town knock on his door and demand sex from the men.

The response from the Levite and his host once again illustrates the utter depravity of the times. Describing their request as "vile" (Judges 19:23), the host offers his virgin daughter. The men refuse and attempt to storm the house. Then the Levite shoves his concubine out into the street where the men rape her all night (vv. 24-26).

The next morning the Levite goes out and sees his concubine fallen on the threshold of the house. He demonstrates no compassion for her, but simply says, "Get up; let's go" (v. 28). She does not respond and is probably already dead. He brings her body back to his hometown where he chops it up into twelve pieces and sends a part to each of the tribes of Israel (v. 29). In this way, the family tragedy becomes a national tragedy.

Repulsed by this great crime, civil war breaks out between Benjamin and the other tribes. In the first battle, God affirmed that the other tribes should go to battle against the Benjamites (20:23), but they lose the battle and suffer many casualties. It may be that God is not really on either side in this battle. Still in the second battle, they defeat the Benjamites (Judges 20).

After the battle is reported, the narrator mentions that the rest of Israel had committed not to give any of their daughters to the Benjamites as wives. In their "righteous indignation," they wanted the whole tribe wiped out, but now they panic that a whole tribe might be lost to Israel (Judges 21:2-3). Their speech and acts reveal just how confused and misguided they are.

Their solution to the problem is convoluted and evil. They regret having taken the oath, but then discover that the people of Jabesh Gilead failed to take the oath, so they feel justified in killing every male and woman who is not a virgin. They then marry off the virgins to the Israelites, but still they are short of the necessary number of women. They then instruct the Benjamites to go to the annual festival at Shiloh and when the virgin girls go out to dance, they are to kidnap them. That way their fathers who took an oath not to marry their daughters to the Benjamites will not technically have broken their oath (vv. 20-22).

What a strange, dark period the time of judges is! Is the book's purpose simply to report this evil? When read at the time of the exile, the book of Judges along with Samuel and Kings will make the reasons for their punishment clear to those who were removed from Israel and forced to live in Babylon. But there is a more immediate purpose to the book that is signaled by the repetitive formula: "In those days Israel had no king; everyone did as they saw fit" (Judges 21:25; see also Judges 17:6; 18:1; 19:1). In other words, the book of Judges reports this horrible situation in order to point to a solution to the problem of moral depravity, spiritual confusion and political fragmentation—kingship.

We should take a look at another book that covers an event from the same period, namely, the book of Ruth. The book of Ruth is a story of loyalty and healing as well as the care of a providential God. The plot starts on a negative note when the family of Elimelek immigrates to the pagan country of Moab to escape a famine in his city, Bethlehem. Elimelek's two sons marry local girls, Orpah and Ruth. Soon, tragedy strikes and Elimelek and his two sons die, leaving Elimelek's wife Naomi and her daughters-in-law to fend for themselves in a world hostile to single women.

A distraught Naomi encourages her daughters-in-law to return home because she has nothing to offer them in Bethlehem, to which she returns. Orpah tearfully returns home, but Ruth pledges her loyalty to Naomi. When they return to Bethlehem, Ruth gleans the fields for food and "just so happens" to work in the fields of Boaz, who turns out to be a close relative. In the "just so happens," we are to see the loyalty of a caring God who works out events to bring Ruth to Boaz's attention. He provides for Ruth and Naomi, and Ruth offers herself to him in marriage (Ruth 3). Boaz hesitates only long enough to assure that another closer relative is willing to pass on the opportunity to marry her himself. The end result is a happy family that produces a child. They name the child Obed, the father of Jesse who is the father of the future King David.

The book reveals that not every story in Israel during the period of Judges was horrible. Interestingly, both books look forward to kingship. In the case of the book of Judges, kingship is seen as the solution to the overwhelming problems of the day. The book of Ruth anticipates David in particular. Future studies will examine how well kingship works out for Israel.

Reading Study Guide

1. Before his death Joshua led the Israelites in a reaffirmation of their covenant with God in which they agree to obey (Joshua 24). According to the book of Judges how well did they do?

2. How would you characterize the Israelites during the period of Judges?

3. Describe the role and purpose of the "judge" in ancient Israel.

4. Do judges always follow one another chronologically?

   Do they rule over all Israel?

5. How do Ehud's left-handedness and Eglon's weight figure into the story?

6. Read Judges 4–5 about Deborah the judge, and write out its structure according to the cycle of the book of Judges.

7. The appendix of the book of Judges has two stories (chaps. 17–18; 19–21) that share a similar structure to one another. What is that structure, and what is the main contribution of these stories to the book of Judges?

8. Are there any good characters in the two stories at the end of the book?

9. Read Judges 17:6; 18:1; 19:1; 21:25. Where does the book of Judges put its hope for a better future?

10. Levities are the priestly tribe set apart for special service to God. Do Levites live up to their holy role in the stories at the end of the book?

What does this tell us about Israel's spiritual state during this period?

11. How does the book of Ruth contribute to a theology of kingship?

⟳ Anticipating the New Testament

Hebrews 11:32-34 mentions a number of judges as examples of faith. Some of these judges have serious moral failings (Samson, for one).

1. How are they models of faith for us today?

In question 9 of this study's "Reading Study Guide," we saw that the book of Judges puts its hope for a better future in kingship. The imperfect deliverers of Judges makes Israel yearn for something better. As we turn to the following studies we will see just how well (or poorly) the kings of Israel and Judah make good on this hope. Judges thus participates in a theology of kingship, and as we read on (see studies 12, 15, and 17) we will see that this theology will lead us to Jesus the Messiah (anointed king).

The Ancient Story and Our Story

As we have seen, the account of the judges follows a fairly strict pattern. The people sin, and God sends an oppressor as judgment. After a while the people repent, and God sends a judge to rescue them. After a period of peace the people sin, and the cycle begins all over again. As we see this pattern work time and time again, we can learn important life lessons. The first is the nexus between sin and judgment. As we will see later when we study the book of Job (study 14), it is not the case that sin automatically and immediately leads to negative consequences. Sin is not the only reason why people experience pain in this life. That said, sin often accounts for our pain, and from a Christian perspective we know that sin does ultimately lead to judgment, that is, unless we repent, which is also a lesson we can learn from the experience of the people who lived during the time of the judges. Repentance brings forgiveness and restoration of relationship with God. Of course, God does not use imperfect deliverers like the judges to rescue us; rather, he sends the perfect king who dies in our place. He is the one who establishes peace in our lives.

LOOKING AHEAD

The period of the judges was a time of spiritual confusion, moral depravity and political fragmentation. While there were some positive moments, God's faithful people desired something better, namely, kingship. As we turn to the next phase, we will observe the transition from judges to kings. We begin with the rise of kingship and the short period of time known as the United Monarchy.

Going Deeper

Schwab, George M. *Right in Their Own Eyes: The Gospel According to Judges*. Phillipsburg, NJ: P & R, 2011.

Younger, K. Lawson. *Judges, Ruth*. NIV Application Commentary. Grand Rapids: Zondervan, 2002.

12 / Saul, David and Solomon

LOOKING AHEAD

MEMORY VERSE: 2 Samuel 7:11b-16
BIBLE STUDY: 1 Samuel 8–12; 15–16; 2 Samuel 7; 1 Kings 3; 11
READING: The Rise of Kingship

 ## Bible Study Guide

After reading 1 Samuel 8–12; 15–16; 2 Samuel 7; 1 Kings 3; 11, spend some time reflecting on these passages with the following questions in mind before looking at the Reading. (For maximum benefit read 1 Samuel 8–1 Kings 11; 1 Chronicles 10–2 Chronicles 9.)

1. Why do the people want a king (1 Samuel 8:4-5), and what are Samuel's and God's reactions?

2. When Samuel anoints Saul as king in private, what does he instruct him to do (1 Samuel 10:1-8)?

   Does he do what Samuel tells him to (1 Samuel 10:9-16)?

3. How does Samuel make Saul's appointment as king public (1 Samuel 10:17-27)?

   How does Saul stand out from other men?

4. What does Saul do that leads to his formal proclamation as king (1 Samuel 11)?

5. Why does Samuel think it important for Israel to renew their covenant commitment to God after Saul is appointed king (1 Samuel 12)?

6. What does Saul do to bring Samuel's and God's anger against him in 1 Samuel 15?

7. Why does God tell Samuel to anoint David (1 Samuel 16:7)?

How does this compare with the choice of Saul?

8. Why does David want to build a house (temple) for God, and why does God reject the idea (2 Samuel 7:1-7)?

9. What does God mean when he tells David that he will "establish a house for you" (2 Samuel 7:11)?

10. What is Solomon's relationship with God like at the beginning of his rule (1 Kings 3)? At the end (1 Kings 11)?

👓 Reading: The Rise of Kingship

In study 11 we observed just how bad things were in Israel. The period of the Judges can be characterized as a period of spiritual confusion, moral depravity and political fragmentation. In the appendix of the book the narrator expresses a desire for kingship as a solution to the problem (for instance, "In those days Israel had no king; everyone did as they saw fit" [Judges 21:25]).

The expectation that Israel would eventually be ruled by a king actually begins early in the history of God's people. God tells Abraham, who was to be the father of many nations, that "kings will come from you" (Genesis 17:6). Later, when Jacob blesses or curses his children, he proclaims concerning Judah that "the scepter [symbolic of kingship] will not depart from Judah, nor the ruler's staff from between his feet" (Genesis 49:10). Balaam, the pagan prophet hired by the king of Moab to curse the Israelites, can only bless them at God's directive, including "their king will be greater than Agag; their kingdom will be exalted" (Numbers 24:7; see also v. 19). Finally, God gives Moses a law that regulates the future institution of kingship in Deuteronomy 17:14-20.

Even with all of this anticipation, however, kingship starts out in a surprising and disturbing way according to 1 Samuel 8–12. The people approach Samuel and ask for a king because they don't trust Samuel and his son, and deeper down

they don't trust God to take care of them. They want a human military leader to help them against their enemies, especially the Philistines ("then we will be like all the other nations, with a king to lead us and to go out before us and fight our battles" [1 Samuel 8:20]). Samuel recognizes their sin in asking for a king, but he takes it personally. God points out that it is really not Samuel that they are rejecting but rather him (1 Samuel 8:7). Nonetheless, God directs Samuel to give them a king. The next few chapters describe the complex and ultimately troubling fashion in which Saul is proclaimed the first king of Israel.

In 1 Samuel 9 the story shifts to Saul, a young man in search of his father's lost donkeys. He cannot find them, so he seeks help from a "man of God," who turns out to be Samuel. When Saul arrives, he is shocked at how he is received by Samuel, but the reader has been informed that the night before God had told Samuel that Saul would be the first king of Israel. Thus, Samuel feasted Saul, and before he left anointed him with olive oil, a symbol of divine appointment to the royal office (1 Samuel 10:1). Indeed, the term *Messiah* means "anointed one" and refers to the appointed king of Israel.

Before Saul leaves Samuel, however, the prophet gives the young man some instructions. He tells Saul what will happen to him after he departs as a way of showing that Samuel is truly a prophet of God and thus his anointing him king is a divine appointment. He says two men will encounter him near Rachel's tomb, and they will tell him that his father is no longer worried about the donkeys but is worried about his son. He will then, according to Samuel, meet three men at the great tree of Tabor, and these three men will be carrying food and offer Saul some. He will then travel on to Gibeah. Now here, significantly, Samuel mentions that there is a garrison of Philistine troops in this town. Their presence probably explains why Samuel calls the city "Gibeah of God," making it all the more offensive that it is occupied by pagan Philistines. When he reaches Gibeah, Samuel says he will meet a group of prophets, and Saul himself will be filled with the Spirit and start prophesying. After all these things happen to Saul, showing him without a doubt that God has truly appointed him leader and has given him the Spirit, Samuel tells him, "Do whatever your hand finds to do, for God is with you" (1 Samuel 10:7). In context this seemingly vague command is quite clear. Saul is to attack the Philistine garrison. Afterward, Saul is to go to Gilgal and wait for Samuel to come.

Everything happens just like Samuel announced. Saul is met by two men at Rachel's tomb who tell him that his father is worried about him. He then encounters three men carrying food who offer it to him. When the band of prophets meets him, Saul begins to prophesy

himself. But then what does Saul do? He goes home and, when asked by his uncle what happened, does not utter a word about what Samuel told him about kingship (1 Samuel 10:16). Saul's start is disappointing indeed.

As a matter of fact, if left to his own, Saul would have spent the rest of his life hidden from public view. Accordingly, Samuel called all Israel to assemble at the town of Mizpah. He then threw lots to determine the tribe (Benjamin), the clan (Matri's), and finally the individual (Saul), whom God had appointed king. Most of the people were pleased with the choice. After all, he was "a head taller than any of the others" (1 Samuel 10:23), but there were some men who doubted his abilities (v. 27).

Finally, Saul demonstrated his abilities when Israel received a message from the people of Jabesh Gilead that they were being subjugated by Nahash the Ammonite. The Spirit of God came on Saul, and he successfully liberated that city. After this, the rise of kingship in Israel reaches a successful conclusion with an important covenant renewal ceremony led by Samuel (1 Samuel 12). The people's request for a king was motivated by a lack of trust in God as their king. Saul had not stepped forward immediately to affirm God's appointment as their first king. The threat was always there that the human king would function not as God's earthly representative but rather as an evil force, oppressing the people and leading them astray. Thus, Samuel directs the people to reaffirm their commitment to follow the Lord. After this, Samuel, the last judge, assumes the position of prophet, one who serves as the conscience of the king, as well as priest.

And Saul needs a conscience. The next story told about the first king underlines his disobedience to the Lord (1 Samuel 13:1-15). Saul and his son Jonathan led the army against the Philistines. As the Philistine army amassed forces to attack Saul, he grew anxious as his troops begin to desert out of fear. Saul was waiting for Samuel to offer the prebattle sacrifices. After all, God would be in their midst fighting for them, so it was necessary to be spiritually prepared before the battle. Saul, as king, was not authorized to offer sacrifices. Samuel could but he was later than expected. Saul then rashly offered the sacrifices, and when Samuel arrived, the prophet-priest was furious. After all, since God fought for Israel, it did not matter how many troops went into the battle. The law even insisted that fainthearted soldiers be allowed to leave the army (Deuteronomy 20:8). As a result, Samuel announced that God would have "established your [Saul's] kingdom over Israel for all time. But now your kingdom will not endure" (1 Samuel 13:13-14). In other words, there would be no Saul dynasty.

Saul never sincerely repents of his sin, and so we are not surprised to find a second story of his disobedience following fast on the first. This time Saul, after a victory, does not do what God commanded concerning his defeated foe. The Amale-

kites had been the first to attack Israel as they left Egypt (Exodus 17:8-15), and as a result God had determined that they feel the full force of his judgment (Deuteronomy 25:17-19). Saul, though, does not carry through on God's instructions, and so now, according to Samuel, "The LORD has torn the kingdom of Israel from you today and has given it to one of your neighbors—to one better than you" (1 Samuel 15:28). The narrative now shifts its attention to David.

Without Saul's knowledge, Samuel goes to Bethlehem on God's orders to anoint a son of a man named Jesse to be the next king of Israel (1 Samuel 16:1-13). The process of selection is revealing, especially when contrasted with the choice of Saul. We might remember that Saul's distinguishing characteristic was his height. So we are not surprised that Jesse brought his sons out one by one beginning with the oldest. God does not choose any of the sons that Jesse brought out to Samuel. When pressed, Jesse mentions that there is yet one more son, the youngest, whom Jesse left tending the sheep, and this is David, the one whom God directs Samuel to anoint. In the process of the selection, God advised Samuel concerning the various sons of Jesse, "Do not consider his appearance or his height, for I have rejected him. The LORD does not look at the things that people look at. People look at the outward appearance, but the LORD looks at the heart" (1 Samuel 16:7).

David does not immediately become king, but he does enter into Saul's service.

Interestingly, the first two stories we hear about the young David are about his role as musician in the court of Saul in order to calm the king's volatile moods and as the one who defeats Goliath (1 Samuel 17). These two stories anticipate David as Israel's psalmist and warrior-king.

As David grows in popularity, Saul grows in his jealousy (1 Samuel 18:9). While Saul takes every opportunity to kill his young rival, David for his part bides his time and does not attempt to depose Saul even when he has the chance (1 Samuel 24; 26). Here David is at his best, waiting on God's timing and not trying to manipulate the fulfillment of the divine promise that he would be the next king. Saul's irrational rage, though, drives him from the court, and he lives for a period of time as a political refugee of sorts. He does, however, have his supporters, including a priest, a prophet and an army of six hundred troops. In a sense, he is a kingdom in exile. In order to avoid Saul, David sought political refuge with, of all people, the Philistines, entering into the service of a Philistine leader named Achish. While he told Achish that he was attacking Israelites, he was actually attacking Israel's enemies.

Eventually, however, Saul comes to a sad end. The Philistines now pressed the battle against him, and he soon discovered that God had abandoned him. He kept trying to get God's guidance by asking the priests to make inquiry, but God was not responding. Saul showed his desperation by going to a medium and asking her to raise Samuel from the dead (1 Samuel 28:3-24), but Samuel simply told him that God was bringing on him the punishment that he, Samuel, had announced when he was alive. Saul was going to die, and the kingdom would pass on to another person, not his son.

In the meantime, David was in a potentially difficult position since his Philistine overlord required him to fight alongside him against the Israelites (1 Samuel 29). However, the other Philistine leaders were fearful that David would turn against them in the midst of the battle. We will never know what David would have done, because Achish reluctantly sent David back to their base in the city of Ziklag. When they got there, they found that Ziklag had been attacked by the hated Amalekites who even took their women. David set off in pursuit of the Amalekites, defeated them and regained what had been lost (1 Samuel 30).

The scene of the narration then shifts again, returning to Saul who was now attacked by the Philistine army. Saul was wounded and feared being taken alive. His armor-bearer refused to finish him off, so Saul killed himself. A tragic end to a sad figure.

When 2 Samuel opens, David hears of the Philistine victory as well as the deaths of Saul and Jonathan his son. Rather than feeling relieved at the death of the man who horribly harassed him, David deeply mourned his death and also the death of his good friend Jonathan (2 Samuel 1).

Not surprisingly, David's home tribe of

Judah immediately recognized him as king (2 Samuel 2:1-7), though the northern tribes under the strong arm of the military leader Abner placed another son of Saul on the throne, a man named Ish-Bosheth. Hostilities immediately erupted between the northern tribes and Judah. The account of the conflict focuses on the personal relationships between Joab (David's general), Abner (the head of Ish-Bosheth's army) and Ish-Bosheth. In the opening skirmish, Abner reluctantly kills a persistent Asahel, Joab's brother, and then encounters the suspicions of the weak king Ish-Bosheth. In response to the latter, Abner brokers a deal with David to turn the kingdom over to him, but before he can do it, Joab murders Abner to avenge the death of his brother Asahel. The narrative goes to great lengths to distance David from responsibility for Abner's murder, thus suggesting that perhaps there were people at the time who suspected him. Without Abner, Ish-Bosheth knew he was in trouble. Likely sensing his weakness, two of his military leaders assassinated Ish-Bosheth and then went and reported it to David. However, they did not get the positive reception that they expected; rather, he had them killed for turning on their master. At every point, the narrative makes it clear that David did not usurp the throne by coercion or assassination.

Even so, David is now proclaimed king of the northern tribes (2 Samuel 5:1-5), and thus all of Israel is united once again under a single king. The next chapters de-scribe the wonderful events of David's early reign. He achieves major military victories, most notably over the Philistines. He conquers Jerusalem from the Jebusites and makes it his capital. He takes steps to make it more than a political center, but also the center of the worship of Yahweh, first by bringing the ark into the city. He then wants to build a permanent worship center, a temple (a house for God), but God does not allow him to do that; rather, God builds a house (a dynasty) for David. (For more on the significance of the temple and David's role, see study 9.) All of this is recorded in 2 Samuel 7, which is commonly known as the chapter that describes the establishment of the Davidic covenant, a covenant of kingship, that will have such an important role in the theology of both the Old and New Testaments (see "Anticipating the New Testament").

David loves God and God loves David and blesses him mightily. Indeed, David is the one who completes the conquest by subduing the last of the internal enemies of Israel. However, an unexpected turn in the story takes place in 2 Samuel 11. Up to this point, David has been the picture of devotion to God and to his law. He has been patient waiting for God to give him the kingdom, refusing to use his own power and control to rush his promised rule over Israel. But now David uses his political power to take another man's wife, Bathsheba, and then covers her pregnancy up by having her husband, Uriah, killed.

Though David repents after being confronted by the prophet Nathan (2 Samuel 12) and God restores his relationship with him, the consequences of his sin are felt for the rest of his reign. Indeed, during the remainder of David's life, he experiences one crisis after another, usually caused by friction within his own family. In the first place, seven days after Bathsheba gave birth, the baby died. Second Samuel 13:1–19:8 give an account of David's son Absalom's rebellion against David. The story begins with another son, Amnon, luring his half-sister, Absalom's sister, into bed and forcing her to have sex. Absalom succeeds in killing Amnon in revenge, after which he seeks refuge in another country. Eventually, Joab, David's general, convinced David to allow Absalom to return to Jerusalem. However, once back, he worked behind his father's back in order to win the affections of the Israelites. Next, he proclaimed himself king, and David had to flee the country. Nonetheless, many stayed loyal to David, and he succeeded in winning the kingdom back. Even though Absalom had betrayed him, David deeply mourned his death. However, almost as soon as the threat from Absalom was resolved, another man, Sheba, tried to tear a part of the kingdom away from David (2 Samuel 20:1-22). David appointed a man named Amasa as the new head of the army to deal with Sheba, but Joab succeeded in assassinating him just as he earlier had assassinated Abner. With the assistance of a wise woman from the city of Abel Beth Maakah, where Sheba had sought refuge, Joab brought this rebellion to a close. These and further problems complicated the end of David's reign, all coming to an end with the turmoil surrounding the succession to the throne. While he had appointed Solomon his heir, another son named Adonijah made a power play for the throne when David was old and infirm (1 Kings 1:1-27). Unfortunately for Adonijah, he had miscalculated David's strength, and the king successfully put Solomon on the throne just before he died.

Solomon is one of the more enigmatic kings of Israel. He starts his reign with great promise and ends a tragic figure. He represents both the heights of wisdom and also the depths of folly. His father, David, accomplished God's will by finishing the conquest and handing his son a unified nation, but Solomon's actions led to its sad division into two parts.

The lion's share of the story of Solomon in Kings focuses on the positive, but even when Solomon's virtues are told, there are anticipations of trouble. After Solomon's throne is established (by executing potential rivals and troublemakers), he travels to Gibeon to offer sacrifices. Why Gibeon? Kings tells us that it "was the most important high place" (1 Kings 3:4), while at the same time informing the reader that "Solomon showed his love for the LORD by walking according to the instructions given him by his father David, except that he offered sacrifices and burned incense on the high places" (v. 3).

Even so, God honored his devotion by

saying, "ask for whatever you want me to give to you" (v. 5), and Solomon pleased God by asking for wisdom ("a discerning heart" [v. 9]). So pleased in fact was God that he also determined to give the king wealth and honor.

Much of the narrative concerning Solomon illustrates and emphasizes his wisdom. Wisdom is the skill of living, "knowing how" rather than "knowing that." A wise person avoids the pitfalls of life and maximizes success. A wise person knows how to say the right thing and do the right thing at the right time. The wise person expresses the right emotion at the right level that is appropriate for the situation at hand (for more on wisdom, see study 14). Most fundamentally, wisdom involves the fear of the Lord. God is the most important and most powerful person in the universe. A wise person listens to God and obeys him.

Solomon certainly demonstrated great wisdom during his life. He showed this in how he ruled his people, making insightful judgments (1 Kings 3:16-28). He amazed neighboring monarchs with his teaching (the Queen of Sheba [1 Kings 10:1-13]) and organized his kingdom efficiently (1 Kings 4:1-28). The author of Kings announced that "God gave Solomon wisdom and very great insight, and a breadth of understanding as measureless as the sand on the seashore" (1 Kings 4:29).

God directed Solomon to build the temple, the symbol of his abiding presence with Israel now that they were permanently established in the land thanks to the warring activity of his father David (see study 9 for more on the temple). In sum, the majority of the story of Solomon emphasizes his wisdom and accomplishments. His reign was characterized by wealth and glory that far exceeded that of David (1 Kings 10:14-29).

Why then was the kingdom split into two parts at the end of his reign? The answer is given in 1 Kings 11, which begins,

> Now King Solomon loved many foreign women. Besides Pharaoh's daughter, he married women from Moab, Ammon, Edom, Sidon, and from among the Hittites. The LORD had clearly instructed the people of Israel, "You must not marry them, because they will turn your hearts to their gods." Yet Solomon insisted on loving them anyway. He had 700 wives of royal birth and 300 concubines. And in fact, they did turn his heart away from the LORD. (1 Kings 11:1-3 NLT)

The result was that God raised up opponents against Solomon; the most significant was a leader of the ten northern tribes, a man named Jeroboam. During Solomon's reign, he had to seek political asylum in Egypt, but once Solomon died, he came back to lead the ten northern tribes in rebellion against Judah and Solomon's son Rehoboam.

Reading Study Guide

1. Judges makes a point of connecting the problems of that day with the lack of a king by repeatedly saying, "In those days Israel had no king; everyone did as they saw fit" (Judges 21:25). How does kingship address the problems of moral depravity, spiritual confusion and political fragmentation?

2. Is kingship a surprise, or was it anticipated in earlier periods? Give the details.

3. Why do you think God gives Israel a king in spite of their sinful request?

4. Describe the relationship between Saul and Samuel the prophet.

   Describe the relationship between David and Nathan the prophet.

   What do these relationships tell you about the character of these two kings?

5. What about Saul made people think he would make a good king?

Why did God think David would make a good king?

6. Why was there a need for a covenant renewal after Saul became king (1 Samuel 12)?

Why did God form a new covenant with David (2 Samuel 7)?

7. What are the great accomplishments of David's kingship?

What are his failures?

8. What role does Joab play in the account of David's kingship?

9. Why does Solomon succeed David on the throne, and not another son?

10. Solomon begins as a wise king and ends a fool. What explains the transformation?

➡ Anticipating the New Testament

In studying the period of the Judges, a time of spiritual confusion, moral depravity and political fragmentation, we observed a deep longing for something better. That hope focused on the institution of kingship, which would provide a strong central leader who could guide the nation morally, spiritually and politically.

Though kingship got off to a rocky start with Saul, David, though not perfect, is depicted as a king whom God loves. Accordingly, God entered into a covenant relationship with David, promising him that he would have a son on the throne forever (2 Samuel 7:11-16). The early Solomon also held much promise as a king who would lead his people toward God and not away from him. Of course, as we have seen, Solomon does not end his reign well, anticipating dark developments in the future.

On the one hand, Saul, David and Solomon begin to illustrate (see also study 15) that kingship does not satisfy the craving for something better that was expressed in the book of Judges. On the other hand, David at his best anticipates what will eventually meet the needs of the people. It is Jesus who will be the fulfillment of the promise to David that he will have a son on the throne forever.

1. In Romans 1:1-7, why does Paul point out that Jesus "was a descendant of David" (v. 3)?

2. How does Jesus fulfill God's promise to David that he will have a descendant on the throne forever?

💬 The Ancient Story and Our Story

The relationship between Saul and David is one of the most compelling stories of the Bible. Why does God reject Saul but embrace David as a model king, even entering into a covenant with him and granting him a dynasty that will last "forever"? After all, both of them on occasion failed to obey God. David, as well as Saul, perpetrated great harm toward others. So what is the difference? In the Reading, I pinpointed the difference in David's willingness to repent. Nothing was more important to him than his relationship with God. Psalm 51, which is identified as a psalm composed by David, articulates the king's deep desire to restore his relationship with God after his sin with Bathsheba.

In this way the narrative underlines the importance of repentance to us. Christians don't stop sinning after they give their lives to Christ. Thus, it is absolutely critical to our Christian growth that we repent of our sins and, with the power of the Spirit, commit ourselves to obedience to God.

The life of Solomon also is an object lesson for Christians today. Even the most spiritually mature among us are vulnerable to a fall. The book of Proverbs, which is associated with Solomon's wisdom in the superscription (Proverbs 1:1), warns young men to avoid romantic connections that will lead them away from a healthy relationship with God. Solomon did not follow this advice and ended up a fool, causing great damage to the people of God as we will see in study 15.

LOOKING AHEAD

Kingship is now established in Israel. Though the stories of David and the early Solomon raise hopes that kingship indeed would resolve the issues of spiritual confusion, moral depravity and political fragmentation, the end of Solomon's reign anticipates dark days ahead. Before turning to the next phase of the history of God's people in the Old Testament in study 15, we will first look at two different types of Old Testament literature associated with David (the Psalms) and Solomon (Wisdom).

Going Deeper

Arnold, Bill T. *1 & 2 Samuel*. NIV Application Commentary. Grand Rapids: Zondervan, 2003.

Boda, Mark J. *After God's Own Heart: The Gospel According to David*. Phillipsburg, NJ: P & R, 2007.

13 / Psalms

LOOKING AHEAD

MEMORY VERSE: Colossians 3:16
BIBLE STUDY: Psalms 1–2; 20; 30; 47; 69; 77; 131; 150
READING: Worshiping the Lord

 **Bible Study Guide**

After reading Psalms 1–2; 20; 30; 47; 69; 77; 131; 150, spend some time reflecting on these passages with the following questions in mind before looking at the Reading. (For maximum benefit read the entire book of Psalms.)

1. The book of Psalms is composed of 150 poems. What are the characteristics of Hebrew poetry that make it different from Hebrew prose?

2. Psalms 1–2 functions like an introduction to the book of Psalms. What subjects do they present to the reader?

3. Describe the people who are blessed according to Psalm 1. What happens to the wicked?

4. What is God's attitude toward earthly powers that resist God's rule according to Psalm 2?

5. According to Psalm 2, what is the relationship between God, the King, and the earthly king?

6. In Psalm 30, why does the psalmist thank God?

   Why did trouble come into his life in the first place?

7. According to Psalm 77:1-6, why did the psalmist's initial remembrance of God only make him feel worse?

8. Is it appropriate to challenge God in the way the psalmist did in Psalm 77:7-12? Why or why not?

9. What event does the psalmist refer to in Psalm 77:16-20?

   Why does he mention it?

10. What about Psalm 150 makes this song an appropriate conclusion to the book as a whole?

👓 Reading: Worshiping the Lord

The book of Psalms may very well be the most beloved part of the Old Testament to Christians today. The 150 poems that comprise the book are heartfelt prayers that help us articulate our own thoughts and feelings to God. John Calvin called the book of Psalms a "mirror of the soul," because they express every possible human emotion, and as we read them they help us to understand what is going on in our own spiritual lives.

The psalms were also set to music and sung by the people of God during worship. The individual psalms were composed and used in a manner similar to our own church hymns. According to the few historical titles of the psalms, it was an experience of God's presence or absence that led to the writing of a sung prayer. For instance, the title of Psalm 51 announces that it was composed "when the prophet Nathan came to him after David had committed adultery with Bathsheba." The content of the psalm, which expresses repentance and seeks forgiveness, fits perfectly with this episode in David's life (see 2 Samuel 11–12). That said, the psalm does not embed the details of the event in the prayer itself. For instance, the psalm does not mention adultery specifically but speaks of sin generally, indicating that this psalm, like all the psalms, was written not to memorialize the event that inspired its writing but to provide a prayer for later worshipers who have similar, though not necessarily identical, issues in their life.

The psalms were written over a period of almost one thousand years. While the largest single group of psalms are identified in their titles as composed by David (c. 1000 B.C.), Psalm 90 is attributed to Moses (from some three to four centuries earlier). The contents of certain psalms (Psalms 126; 127) seem at home in the exilic or postexilic period (sixth century B.C. or after).

The structure of the final form of the book of Psalms has been a matter of discussion. While some detect a detailed and meaningful outline to the final form of the book, the lack of agreement about the precise shape of its organization makes it more likely that the precise order of the psalms is not significant. Of course, there are small collections of psalms that seem to have entered the collection as a group. One of the most interesting is the "songs of ascents" (Psalms 120–134). These songs were used as people journeyed to "go up" to Jerusalem to celebrate one of the great annual festivals (Passover, Booths, Pentecost).

While an overarching structure to the book is unlikely, it appears that Psalms 1 and 2 are placed at the beginning of the book to serve as a kind of introduction. Psalm 1 begins by pronouncing a blessing on people who avoid association with wicked people (v. 1). The focus is rather on the "law of the LORD" (v. 2), and as a result they grow like a tree planted by water. On the other hand, the wicked are like rootless chaff blowing in the wind. Psalm 1 invites its readers to reflect on which side of this divide they are on. The implicit message is that only the righteous can proceed into the intimate fellowship with God afforded by the psalms.

Indeed, the book of Psalms is like a literary sanctuary. The sanctuary, or holy place, could only be entered by the righteous, not the wicked (see Psalms 15; 24:3-4), and was protected by priestly gatekeepers (1 Chronicles 26:1-19). Psalm 1 functioned as a gatekeeper to the psalms, requiring its readers to identify either with the blessed righteous or the rejected wicked. Once the righteous entered the sanctuary of the book of Psalms, they encountered the second psalm with its majestic picture of God and his anointed one. The rebellious kings of the earth (v. 2) are no match for God the heavenly king (v. 4) and his messiah or anointed one. When first composed, the messiah was David and his descendants, God's royal representatives on earth, as is indicated by the citation of 2 Samuel 7:14 in Psalm 2:7. The psalm was likely used as a coronation hymn. However, once the Davidic dynasty came to an end, this psalm, as well as the other royal psalms, evoked expectations of the coming of a future son of David who would rule on the throne. Of course, the New Testament understands this expectation to be fulfilled in Jesus, the *Christ* (the Greek equivalent of Messiah).

Psalms 1–2, thus, serves as a preamble to the book, introducing two important themes, law and messiah. No strict order can be observed in the many psalms that follow. That said, a careful reader can see that while the first part of the book majors on laments, the concluding part of the book emphasizes hymns of praise. In other words, there is a movement from sadness to joy in the Psalms. This growing celebration reaches a climax in the final five psalms (146–150), which serve as a fitting conclusion to the book. A quick glance at these five psalms shows a recurring phrase, "praise the Lord" (Hebrew *Hallelujah*). The final psalm culminates this giant doxology by calling on Israel to praise God some thirteen times. What a fitting way to leave the literary sanctuary of the Psalms, singing praises to God!

While the book of Psalms is composed of 150 different songs, they fall into distinct categories. None are exactly alike, but it is still helpful to recognize that there are seven basic types of psalms, three major and four minor.

The three major types are hymns, laments and thanksgiving psalms. The hymns are songs of joy, sung when everything is going right with life. The psalmist loves God, other people and himself. Psalm 98 is an excellent example of a hymn that celebrates God as the one who has given them a victory in the past (vv. 1-3), is their King in the present (vv. 4-6) and will come as judge in the future (vv. 7-9).

The lament is a fitting prayer when life falls apart. The psalmist expresses disappointment in God, other people and even himself. Psalm 69 is a good example of a lament. The psalmist begins by invoking God to come help him (v. 1; see also vv. 13-18). He continues by describing his complaint (vv. 2-4, 7-12, 19-21). In this lament he confesses his sin (v. 5), but in others the psalmist protests his innocence (Psalm 26). Some, but not all, laments are similar to Psalm 69 in the presence of curses against the psalmist's enemies (Psalm 69:22-28). Almost all laments (but see Psalm 88) turn at the end to praise or express confidence in God.

The third major type of psalm is thanksgiving psalms, which are sung when God hears a lament and answers it. Psalm 30 provides an excellent example, in which the psalmist praises God for healing him from a near mortal illness.

The four minor categories are psalms of confidence, wisdom psalms, royal psalms and remembrance psalms. Psalms of confidence, as their name implies, are prayers where the psalmist expresses his deep-seated trust in God. Psalm 131 is an excellent example. The psalmist calls on Israel to hope in the Lord after he himself has stilled and quieted his soul to the point that his relationship with God is like that of a mother with a weaned child. Wisdom psalms share the vocabulary, concepts and themes of wisdom literature (Proverbs, Job, Ecclesiastes and Song of Songs; see study 14). Psalm 1, which I described earlier, is a wisdom psalm using the vocabulary and themes of Proverbs, including the division between the righteous and the wicked, and describing the positive consequences that will come to the

former and the negative ones to the latter. Psalm 73 is a second example, treating, like Job, the question of the suffering of the righteous.

Remembrance plays a major role in all the different types of poems found in the book of Psalms. Psalm 77, for instance, is a lament that finds confidence for the present and hope for the future in remembrance of God's "deeds." At the end the psalmist in particular remembers the crossing of the Sea at the time of the exodus. That said, there are a handful of psalms in which remembrance of the past is the major theme. A good example is Psalm 136, which praises God as it surveys all the wonderful acts he has performed for the benefit of humanity and in particular his people. The psalm is also clearly a liturgical song where the priest would intone the first part of a verse and the congregation would respond with "His love endures forever." After a general introduction (vv. 1-4), the priest begins by remembering God's act of creation (vv. 5-9), and then continues by citing the exodus (vv. 10-15) and wilderness wandering and conquest (vv. 16-22) before concluding with praise and thanks (vv. 23-26). Finally, while kingship is a theme that appears in many psalms, it is the major concern of a number of psalms. There are divine kingship psalms as well as those that pray for God's human representative, the king of Israel. Psalm 47 is a good example of the former, describing God assuming his throne amid the praise of his subjects. Psalm 20, a prayer asking for support for the human king, illustrates the latter type. Psalm 2, already discussed, speaks of both the divine king as well as his human representative, the messiah.

To understand the Psalms well, a reader should know how poetry functions in the Old Testament. The first characteristic of poetry in the Old Testament, obvious just by looking at the page, is that the lines are very short. In a word, poetry packs a lot of meaning in just a few words. That means careful readers should take their time and reflect on the poem. Poetry should not be skimmed but meditated upon.

Further, rather than being formed by sentences that group into paragraphs, poetry is made up of short clauses (often called "cola") that form lines. These lines are typically either two-part (a bicolon) or three-part (a tricolon). Each colon of a parallel line furthers the thought of the first line. The second colon is always "more than" the first colon. For instance, take Psalm 131:1:

> My heart is not proud, Lord,
>   my eyes are not haughty;
> I do not concern myself with great
>   matters
>   or things too wonderful for me.

This verse contains two closely related bicola. In the first colon the psalmist denies pride in his heart, while the second denies it in his eyes. The poet thus deftly moves from the inside (his heart) to the outside, the way he appears to the world (his eyes). In the second bicolon, he continues his denial of arrogance, but now he moves to his ambition. The second colon intensifies or sharpens the thought of the first by using a rarer, more expressive word. The first word is a common word for "great matters," while the second, "wonderful things," could almost be translated miraculous things. When we read poetry in the Old Testament, it is good to be sensitive to the development within the poetic lines.

The poetry of the Psalms is also notable for its use of vivid imagery. Metaphors and similes stimulate the imagination of readers. Images of God and his relationship to his people are particularly compelling. God is a shepherd of his sheep (Psalm 23), a king praised by his subjects (Psalm 47), a warrior who rescues his people (Psalm 7), a mother of his people who are likened to a weaned child (Psalm 131), and the list goes on and on. Such imagery compares God to something in the reader's experience and requires us to reflect and unpack the relationship between the two parts of the image.

While compact language, parallelism and imagery are the leading features of Hebrew poetry, the psalmist had many other literary tools at his disposal to make his composition memorable and interesting as well as informative. Many of these tools are hidden from those who read the psalms in English translation since, for instance, sound plays and word plays only make sense in Hebrew. For instance, a few psalms are written in what is called an acrostic structure. That is, the poet will write a poem so that each unit will begin with a successive letter of the Hebrew alphabet (Psalms 9–10; 111; 112; 119). English readers may be familiar with this feature in Psalm 119, a poem that is divided into twenty-two stanzas of eight verses each, each verse in each stanza starting with a successive letter of the Hebrew alphabet. Most English translations place the relevant letter at the beginning of each stanza. An acrostic signals to the reader that the poet is given a full (A to Z, so to speak) treatment of a topic, the law in the case of Psalm 119.

Through its use of poetry the book of Psalms not only informs our intellect, it also arouses our emotions, stimulates our imagination and appeals to our will. Good reading of the psalms requires not only knowledge of the way poetry works in the Old Testament but also patience to reflect carefully on the beautiful and meaningful poetic language.

As we observed in the description of imagery in the psalms, we learn a lot about the nature of God and our relationship with him from this book. Almost every psalm contains at least one striking image of who God is. The book is like a verbal portrait gallery of God and should be studied to learn more about God as well as ourselves.

Besides revealing God and anticipating Jesus, the psalms also help us express our heart in prayer to God. No matter what we are feeling inside—love, hate, anger, joy, depression, envy, generosity—there is a psalm that expresses that emotion. Indeed, reading the psalms will help us discover what we are feeling inside, in this way operating as a "mirror of the soul." But the psalms do more than help us understand ourselves; they also minister to us. Let's say we are depressed and we find ourselves drawn to Psalm 130, which begins, "Out of the depths I cry to you, LORD." By the end of the psalm, this lament has moved from sadness to a confident assertion that God "himself will redeem Israel from all their sins."

The psalms not only inform us about God and influence our emotions in positive directions, they also shape our attitudes and guide our actions. Here there is overlap with the function of the psalms as a "mirror of the soul," since the psalms not only intend to tell the reader how they are doing "on the inside," but also to change attitude and behavior. The psalms are frequently explicit in their goals for the reader through the use of imperatives. Psalm 131 is a good example. After the psalmist describes his own sure trust in God in the midst of trouble, he ends by calling on Israel to "hope in the LORD." Such is the attitude that the psalmist wants to move the reader toward.

A quick survey of the psalms will reveal that many of the imperatives of the psalms concern worship. After all, the primary use of the psalms during the Old Testament period was in corporate worship. The psalmist calls on his readers/hearers to "worship the LORD," "shout joyfully to him" and most of all and climactically to "praise him." In a word, the psalms move readers to an enthusiastic and participatory worship of God.

Reading Study Guide

1. Why are many Christians attracted to the book of Psalms more than other parts of the Old Testament?

2. What does it mean to read the Psalms as a mirror of the soul? Read Psalm 130 as a mirror of your soul.

3. Why don't the psalms specify the particular historical event(s) that led to their composition?

   How does this help us apply the psalms to our lives?

4. Explain what is meant when we say that the book of Psalms is like a sanctuary.

5. Read Psalm 3. What type (genre) of psalm is it?

What about Psalms 7, 23, 46, 73?

6. Reflect on the parallel lines in Psalm 6:1-2. How is the B line "more than" the A line?

7. Read Psalm 78:65 and unpack the unusual imagery in this verse.

8. Read Psalm 88 and describe the emotions expressed by the psalmist.

9. Examine Psalm 58 for imprecations. How should Christians approach curses like these?

➔ Anticipating the New Testament

Christians read the book of Psalms in the light of the coming of Christ. Indeed, Jesus encourages such a reading in Luke 24:44 when he told his disciples that he is spoken of in "the Law of Moses, the Prophets and the Psalms." Sometimes Christ is anticipated in a psalm because he fulfills the image of God presented in the poem. For instance, when Christians read Psalm 23, they cannot help but think of Jesus who is "the good shepherd" (John 10:1-21). Or think of the many psalms that speak of the king. For instance, Psalm 2, which talks about the nations that rage against the "LORD and against his anointed" (v. 2). Of course, the New Testament presents Jesus as the ultimate anointed (Messiah/Christ), the fulfillment of the Davidic promise that a son of David would be on the throne forever (2 Samuel 7:16).

In addition, since Jesus is God himself, the psalms are rightly prayed to Jesus. We share our joys, our problems, our thanks and our confidence through the psalms with Jesus.

Finally, it is often helpful to read a psalm as if Jesus himself is praying it. Indeed, sometimes the New Testament reports that Jesus prays the psalms to express his feelings. Note, for instance, Matthew 27:45-46, which quotes Psalm 22:1. But the psalm does not have to be quoted in the New Testament for it to be understood as a prayer of Jesus. Psalm 131 provides a good example. As the psalmist expresses his lack of pride and the manner in which he stilled and quieted his heart, we can think of Jesus himself as the ultimate example of this attitude. Indeed, reading the psalm as if Jesus himself prayed it evokes a picture of Jesus in the Garden of Gethsemane calming his anxiety and submitting his will to his Father's purposes.

1. How does Psalm 8 anticipate Jesus Christ?

2. How does Psalm 110 anticipate Jesus?

3. Pray Psalm 51 as a prayer to Jesus.

● The Ancient Story and Our Story

As mentioned earlier, the book of Psalms is perhaps the most beloved part of the Old Testament to people of faith today. The reason may be found in the concept of Calvin's "mirror of the soul." While the psalms were written by an author inspired by his or her own experience of God's presence or absence in a concrete event, they were written in such a way that others who use the psalm as a model prayer can apply it to their own similar, though not necessarily identical, situation. Thus, the psalms are a resource of prayer for God's people as they express their joys, sorrows, thanks and confidence to God. When we have difficulty articulating our feelings, the psalms will help us find words to express ourselves to God, and to do so honestly. The psalms hold nothing back from God and thus encourage us to be ruthlessly honest in our prayers.

We can tell God everything that is on our hearts, even our anger and disappointment in him. In short, the psalms provide a tutorial on how we should pray to God.

We should also not lose sight of the fact that the psalms are not in the first place private prayers but rather the hymnbook of the Old Testament people of God. They were written to be sung corporately. Thus, the psalms encourage us toward enthusiastic and sincere worship.

The psalms also form our understanding of the nature of God. He is the Shepherd, the King, the Warrior, the Mother and on and on. We do well to reflect on these picture images of God in order to enter into a more intimate relationship with him. As we have also just seen, the psalms anticipate Christ and thus, along with the New Testament, we should read the psalms as foreshadows of our Savior.

LOOKING AHEAD

Before returning to the next phase of the history of God's people (see study 15), we will first explore wisdom literature, a type of writing associated mainly with King Solomon.

Going Deeper

Longman, Tremper, III. *How to Read the Psalms*. Downers Grove, IL: InterVarsity Press, 1988.

14 / Wisdom

MEMORY VERSE: Proverbs 1:7
BIBLE STUDY: Proverbs 1; 8; 9; 10; Job 1–3; 11–13; 38; 42; Ecclesiastes 1–2; 12;
Song of Songs 4:1–6:3
READING: Navigating the Turbulent Waters of Life

 ## Bible Study Guide

After reading Proverbs 1; 8; 9; 10; Job 1–3; 11–13; 38; 42; Ecclesiastes 1–2; 12; Song of Songs 4:1–6:3, spend some time reflecting on these passages with the following questions in mind before looking at the Reading. (For maximum benefit read Job, Proverbs, Ecclesiastes and Song of Songs in their entirety.)

1. Proverbs 1:2-7 is the preface to the book as a whole. What does this text tell you about the purpose of the book?

   Based on these verses, how would you describe wisdom?

2. Proverbs 9:1-6, 13-18 present two women issuing an invitation to young men to join them for dinner. After also reading Proverbs 8, what or who do you think Woman Wisdom represents?

   What about Woman Folly?

   Why do the young men have to make a choice between them?

3. In Proverbs 10 we have the first of a number of chapters that list proverbs that make observations and give instructions concerning a variety of subjects. Make a list of the subjects addressed.

4. Why does Job 1–2 put such a big emphasis on Job's integrity?

   Why do the three friends react so negatively to Job's comments in chapter 3?

5. Job 11–13 is one of many interchanges between Job and his three friends, in this case Zophar. What is Zophar's main point concerning Job's suffering?

   What does he think Job needs to do to escape his suffering?

6. How would you characterize God's reaction to Job once he finally speaks to him in chapter 38?

   How does Job ultimately respond to God's speeches (Job 42:1-6)?

7. Notice the shift in speaker between Ecclesiastes 1:1-11 and verse 12 and following in the book of Ecclesiastes (from "the Teacher, he" to "I, the Teacher"). What does that tell you about the number of speakers in the book?

8. In Ecclesiastes 2:1-23 the Teacher tries to find meaning in pleasure, then wisdom, then work. What is his conclusion?

What do you think the Teacher meant by the phrase "under the sun" (Ecclesiastes 2:17 and repeated a number of times in the book)?

9. Notice the same shift in speaker that we observed in Ecclesiastes 1 between Ecclesiastes 12:7 and verse 8. What does the Teacher say about death in 12:1-7?

What are the conclusions drawn about the Teacher in 12:8-14?

10. What is the poem in Song of Songs 4:1–5:1 telling us about the attitude of the book toward sexuality?

11. What message is the poet delivering about sexuality by having the man and the woman struggle toward intimacy in Song of Songs 5:2–6:3?

Reading: Navigating the Turbulent Waters of Life

To understand why Job, Proverbs, Ecclesiastes and Song of Songs are considered wisdom books in the Old Testament, we must begin by exploring the nature of wisdom. Wisdom is different than intelligence. Intelligence is a knowledge of facts, a "knowing that," while wisdom is more like a skill, a skill of living, a "knowing how" to navigate life. Wisdom involves the ability to avoid the problems of life and to get out of problems when they arise. Wisdom includes the ability to say the right thing at the right time, to do the right thing at the right time, and to feel and express the right emotion at the right level that is appropriate to the situation. From this description we can see that timing is a very important concept to biblical wisdom.

The book of Proverbs gives the clearest exposition of biblical wisdom in the Old Testament, so we will begin our study there. Proverbs gets its name from the many proverbs that are found in the book, particularly in the second part (chaps. 10–31). A proverb is a short observation, admonition or warning given in a witty, memorable form (especially in the Hebrew) that captures an essential truth. Most English speakers are familiar with our own proverbs that fit this definition. Examples include "haste makes waste" and "the early bird catches the worm." Proverbs 10:1, 4 will serve as examples of biblical proverbs:

A wise son brings joy to his father,
　but a foolish son brings grief to
　　his mother.

Lazy hands make for poverty,
　but diligent hands bring wealth.

While it is right to begin our understanding of biblical wisdom with the idea of skill of living, it would be wrong to end there. The final verse of the prologue to the book (Proverbs 1:7) makes it clear that biblical proverbs are much deeper than simply knowing how to navigate life:

The fear of the LORD is the
　　beginning of knowledge,
　but fools despise wisdom and
　　instruction.

In other words, one cannot claim to be wise if he or she does not have the right attitude toward God, namely, fear. This fear is not the type that makes one run away, but it entails an acknowledgement that God is in charge. We cannot be wise in and of ourselves ("in our own eyes" [Proverbs 3:7]), but only as we listen to the teaching provided by God himself, which is contained in the book of Proverbs.

Accordingly, the wisdom of the individual proverbs that seems like practical advice is actually deeply theological. Besides the clear statement of Proverbs 1:7, the theological dimension of wisdom may be observed in the figure of Woman Wisdom in the first nine chapters of the book. While the second part of the book (chaps. 10–31) is composed of proverbs, the first part (chaps. 1–9) contains longer discourses, typically of a father to his son, but occasionally of a woman named Wisdom who speaks to all the young men. While the father and Woman Wisdom address a number of important issues, most notably sexuality, the path, which stands for life's journey, is the most frequently repeated metaphor. There are two paths, and the goal of the instruction is to keep the young men on the straight, smooth, well-lit path that leads to life and off the twisty, pot-filled, dark path that leads to death. The former is the path of wisdom, godliness and righteousness, while the latter is the path of folly, ungodliness and wickedness.

The climax of the first nine chapters takes place when the path leads the reader (who identifies with the young son) to a place where he receives an invitation sent by the Woman named Wisdom from her grand house located on "the highest point of the city" (Proverbs 9:3) to join her for a meal (vv. 1-6). To dine with someone is an invitation to an intimate relationship. Woman Wisdom wants her hearers to make her an integral part of their life. At the end of the chapter the reader receives a second invitation, this time from a woman named Folly, whose house is also said to be "at the highest point of the city" (v. 14). The reader must decide whom he will dine with and enter into a deep relationship with.

Who are these women? We should take our cue from the location of their houses on the heights, where in the ancient Near East, including Israel, the temple was located. Thus, Woman Wisdom represents Yahweh, the God of Israel, the true God, while Woman Folly stands for the false gods of the nations who try to lead the Israelites astray. We can conclude that the concept of wisdom is more than just practical skill; it involves a relationship with Yahweh, the true God. Folly then involves a relationship with false gods.

The reader of Proverbs is to carry this theological understanding of wisdom into the second part of the book. If read in isolation, the individual proverbs seem secular or "just so much good advice," but read in the context of chapters 1–9, they are theological.

We can illustrate this point with comments on Proverbs 10:1, 4. In verse 1, the wise child, who brings joy to his father, is acting like a true worshiper of Yahweh, while the foolish child, who brings grief to his mother, is acting like an idolater. In verse 4, the hard worker (clearly advocated as wise behavior) is wise and thus acting like a proper worshiper of the true God, while a lazy person is a fool who acts like the follower of false gods.

Before leaving Proverbs, we need to consider two other issues that help shape our understanding of proverbs that are frequently misunderstood, leading to faulty interpretation and application. The first important feature of a proverb we must bear in mind is that they are not always true, but are only true when they are applied at the right time. In the very first paragraph of this essay I indicated that timing is everything when it comes to wisdom. Just knowing a proverb but not being sensitive to when it is relevant to a situation is useless knowledge (Proverbs 26:7), even dangerous (Proverbs 26:9). A clear example that a proverb is not always true comes from Proverbs 26:4-5:

> Do not answer a fool according to
>   his folly,
>   or you yourself will be just like
>   him.
> Answer a fool according to his folly,
>   or he will be wise in his own eyes.

Well, which is it? Should we answer foolish arguments or not? It depends on the circumstance the wise person finds him- or herself in. Is the foolish person teachable? Are there other people around who might benefit from a response even if the person himself will not listen?

The second important feature of a proverb to bear in mind is that the rewards and punishments connected to wise and foolish behavior are not guarantees but rather informing us what the best route to a desired conclusion is, all other things being equal. I will illustrate with Proverbs 10:4. It is generally true in the vast majority of cases that laziness leads to poverty. When people are lazy, they will lose their jobs and end up penniless. However, in Old Testament times as well as today, a lazy person might be born into wealth, inheriting vast amounts of money. Does this person's inheritance render Proverbs 10:4 false? No, because proverbs do not make promises.

That said, readers, ancient and modern, have a tendency to treat these rewards and punishments as promises (see "The Ancient Story and Our Story" on the prosperity gospel). This tendency underlines the importance of reading the book of Proverbs along with our second wisdom book, Job.

Job is one of the best-known books of the Old Testament, being the story of a man who is innocent but nonetheless suffers greatly. The question of why the innocent suffer and evil people prosper has plagued humanity through history down to the present day.

A brief overview of the book begins with the prologue (Job 1–2), where all the main characters, except one (Elihu), are introduced. Job is an innocent, godly and wise man, who at the beginning of the story is blessed with riches and a large, happy family, as one might suspect from the connection between wisdom and reward we saw in the book of Proverbs. The Accuser (the Satan) challenges God that Job's relationship with him is based on the reward pure and simple, a view that God rejects. So God allows the Accuser to bring harm into Job's life, first removing all that he holds dear to him (Job 1:13-19) and then afflicting his body (Job 2:7-8). In spite of these tests, Job remains faithful to God. At the end of the prologue, Job's three friends arrive and sit with him in silence for seven days.

In Job 3, Job himself breaks the silence by uttering a complaint that he wished he had never been born. This complaint has similarities with the laments of the psalms, but shows differences that are significant, the most important of which is that his words are not addressed to God. Unlike the lament psalms, Job's complaint indicates no hope that God will make things better.

At this point the three friends jump into action. They argue with Job in a debate over the cause of Job's suffering as well as what he should do to get out of his current wretched condition. In other words, the three friends act like wise men who can help another person navigate life. Their counsel is based on their belief that suffering is always the result of sin. Thus, the mere fact that Job suffered so horribly is a sure sign that Job is a flagrant sinner. This viewpoint, known as retribution theology, leads them to instruct Job to repent in order to restore his previous blessed condition. Job responds to their charges by vehemently denying that he is a sinner. Interestingly, he shares their view of retribution theology, but since he knows he is not a sinner, he believes God is unjust to punish him. He thus believes that the only remedy for his pain is to confront God and set him straight. This debate between Job and his three friends comprises the largest single part of the book (chaps. 4–27), though it does not lead to any kind of resolution. The three friends run out of steam, but Job continues on.

He begins by rehearsing a powerful poem on the wisdom of God (Job 28). As we will note later, this poem, which basically says that all wisdom is God's wisdom, anticipates the most important conclusion of the book of Job. One expects the book to

end with this affirmation, but Job slides back into the despair of his pain, and he goes on in his monologue with a wistful remembrance of his former blessed life and then contrasts it with his present pitiful existence (Job 29–30). He finds this situation unfair, and so he concludes his speech with a vehement protest of innocence (Job 31), asserting his confident belief that if he could only confront God, he would exonerate himself (vv. 35-37).

At this point in the story we expect to hear from God, but instead a hitherto unintroduced character speaks, a man named Elihu. He first accuses the three friends of not properly interacting with Job, since Job still maintains his view that he is innocent and undeserving of punishment. While the three friends represent human wisdom based primarily on tradition, authority and age, Elihu is a young man who claims spiritual inspiration for his insight (Job 32:8). With all his bluster, Elihu just continues the arguments of the friends, reasserting the theology of retribution that claims that sufferers are sinners. As a result, his arguments are completely ignored by Job as well as God.

We come to the apex of the book of Job when God speaks to Job out of the whirlwind (Job 38:1). God begins by questioning Job concerning his knowledge of the cosmos and nature, beginning with "Where were you when I laid the earth's foundation?" (v. 4), a question which of course Job cannot answer, nor can he answer any of the questions God peppers him with. God is not expecting answers; he is making the point that Job's wisdom is severely limited. Thus, he should not challenge God as he has been doing. While Job responds to God's first speech by silencing himself (Job 40:4-5), God is not yet satisfied, so he delivers a second speech that begins with the question, "Would you discredit my justice? Would you condemn me to justify yourself?" (v. 8). Job had been accusing God of injustice in allowing him to suffer even though he is not a sinner. God challenges such an accusation and then asserts his power and wisdom again by talking about his (and not Job's) mastery over the most powerful land (Behemoth) and sea (Leviathan) creatures known to humanity. In his second response, Job now repents (Job 42:1-6), and after he provides sacrifices on behalf of his three friends, God restores him (vv. 7-17).

Notice that Job never learns why he suffered, and thus the book is not really about suffering. Readers learn some lessons about suffering to be sure. It undermines the idea that all suffering is the result of sin. When we suffer, we cannot assume it is a punishment for something that we did wrong. Ultimately the cause of our suffering remains a mystery. The book of Job is about wisdom as well as how we should suffer. All the human characters set themselves as teachers of wisdom able to solve the problems of life. But they all fail, and at the end of the book God demonstrates that he is the source of all wisdom. The message is that when we suffer, we may not be able to figure out why. We often cannot fathom a way out of our suffering.

How then should we suffer? Certainly God permits us to question him as Job did throughout the dialogues (see also the lament psalms), but ultimately God wants us to bow before him and trust him even when we don't have the answers.

As we turn to the third wisdom book in the Old Testament, we will see that Ecclesiastes too raises the question of the relationship between our behavior and the quality of life (retribution theology), but this issue is not the main theme of the book. Ecclesiastes most notably raises the important question of the meaning, or purpose, of life.

To understand the message of the book, we must first recognize that there are two speakers. The first voice is that of "the Teacher," who speaks in the large middle section of the book (Ecclesiastes 1:12–12:7). He speaks in the first person ("I") as he explores life to discover its meaning. As he looks at work, wisdom, money, power, fame and pleasure as potential sources of meaning, he famously concludes "meaningless, meaningless, everything is meaningless." In brief, the Teacher concludes that life is difficult and then we die. Indeed, he believes that life is meaningless for three reasons. The first is because we die, and since he does not believe in the afterlife, death renders every accomplishment in life meaningless. The second reason is injustice. Life is not fair. The righteous, godly person suffers, and the wicked person prospers. The third feature of life that frustrates the Teacher's goal of discovering meaning in life is the inability to discern the proper time. In our previous discussion of Proverbs we saw that wise living depends on timing. The Teacher knows that God made everything for a proper time (Ecclesiastes 3:1-8), but unfortunately God does not let us read the time so we do the right thing or say the right thing (vv. 9-15). In the absence of meaning or purpose in life, the Teacher advocates finding enjoyment whenever and wherever one can. In other words, *carpe diem*, seize the day (Ecclesiastes 2:24-26)!

The Teacher delivers a pretty depressing message, but it is important not to confuse his teaching with the teaching of the book of Ecclesiastes. The second voice, that of an unnamed wise man, frames the Teacher's words. This wise man is talking in the third person ("the teacher, he . . ." [Ecclesiastes 12:9-10]) about the Teacher to his son (v. 12). He is using the Teacher's ideas to teach his son about what is really important in life. In the first part of the epilogue (Ecclesiastes 12:8-12), he explains that it is important that his son hears what the Teacher has to say. After all "the Teacher searched to find just the right words, and what he wrote was upright and true" (v. 10). What truths did he express? The Teacher rightly described life "under the sun," that is apart from God. Apart from God, life is difficult and then we die. The ultimate purpose of life is not found in work, money, pleasure or any of the other areas that the Teacher explored. That is why the second wise man points his son to an "above the sun" perspective

on life. At the very end of the book he concludes by telling his son,

> Here is the conclusion of the
>   matter:
> Fear God and keep his
>   commandments,
>   for this is the duty of all
>   mankind.
> For God will bring every deed into
>   judgment,
>   including every hidden thing,
>   whether it is good or evil.
>   (Ecclesiastes 12:13-14)

In short, put God first. Have the right relationship with him (fear God), maintain that relationship by obeying his commands and live in the light of the coming judgment. We find true meaning in God, and after that everything else (work, money, etc.) can find its proper place.

The final book that I will treat as wisdom is the Song of Songs. We could have easily treated the Song along with the Psalms as lyric poetry, but on the principle that wisdom concerns God's guidance to life, the Song, which speaks about sexuality, can also be considered wisdom literature.

While some readers believe that the Song is telling a story about a particular couple, it is much more likely that the Song is a collection or anthology of love poems. The poems share much in common and were likely written by a single author, though the book does not have a plot. The poems should be enjoyed as poetry that expresses emotions and uses exciting and often provocative imagery.

The primary theme of the Song is simply the celebration of sexuality. Song of Songs 4:1–5:1 illustrates this theme. Here the man praises the woman's beauty as he describes her from head down. After describing her eyes, hair, teeth, lips, cheeks, neck and breasts, he eventually waxes eloquently about her garden (Song 4:12-15). The garden is exotic with rare and costly spices in the middle of which is a fountain. This image is seen elsewhere in ancient Near Eastern love poetry and refers to the most private and erotic part of the woman's body. In short, this poem is a prelude to lovemaking.

While the man notes that the woman's garden has been private and secluded (v. 12), the woman opens up her garden to the man (v. 16). He happily enters the garden and enjoys its fruit (Song 5:1).

The next poem (Song 5:2–6:3) speaks to another theme of the Song, the fact that intimacy is not easily achieved. In this poem the woman awakes to hear the man knocking on her door. Again, we here encounter another well-known ancient Near Eastern image. A woman opening her door to a man represents sexual intimacy. In this poem the woman initially refuses to open the door to the man, but after a while she is aroused and goes to the door, only to find that he has left. The point is that when the man is ready for intimacy, she is not, and when she is ready, he isn't.

The woman sets out to find him. Her desire even propels her to ignore social custom (represented by the watchmen who try to prevent her from searching for him). She enlists other young women to help her and in the process offers a description of his physical beauty just as he had done for her in chapter 4. The poem ends with the anticipation that they will eventually be reunited in the gardens (Song 6:2-3).

In the context of the Bible as a whole, the Song is about the redemption of sexuality. As we saw in the first study, when Adam and Eve were created, they were naked and felt no shame. However, in the second study, on Genesis 3, we noted that sin marred relationship, so they could not stand exposed to each other without feeling shame. The Song describes a man and a woman in the garden naked and feeling no shame—at least most of the time. In spite of sin, an intimate relationship between a man and a woman is still possible.

Finally, we can speak of another important theological dimension to this human love poem. Throughout the Bible, God's relationship with his people is likened to a marriage. Granted, most of the time this metaphor is used in a negative fashion, but the negative presumes the positive, that is, Israel is God's wife. In Hosea 1 and 3, and Ezekiel 16 and 23, the wife has committed adultery, but a passage like Jeremiah 2:2-3 speaks of how Israel was a bride who was "eager to please" God. The point is that as we read the Song and reflect on the exclusive, passionate, intimate nature of the relationship between the man and the woman, we are also learning about an important dimension of our relationship with God.

Reading Study Guide

1. Describe biblical wisdom in your own words. Give examples from your own life of wise behaviors or decisions that you have made.

2. The book of Proverbs speaks of a father who instructs his son. How should women apply this book to their lives?

3. Proverbs 10 is typical of chapters 10–31 in that the topics seem random in their organization. Can you think of a reason why the book would display this rather arbitrary structure?

4. In the Reading we discussed how the book of Job undermines retribution theology. Define retribution theology. Is retribution theology still around today?

5. The book of Job helps us think through how we should react when we suffer. How would you summarize the book's message on this subject?

6. The main message of the book of Ecclesiastes is to put God first. Does that mean that work, pleasure, wisdom and money have no value at all?

7. The Song of Songs is a book that focuses on physical intimacy between a man and a woman. Why would there be a whole book on sex in the Bible?

Anticipating the New Testament

The whole New Testament proclaims that Jesus is wise in the sense that the book of Proverbs uses the term *wisdom* (see, for example, Mark 1:21-22; 6:2; Luke 2:40-50; 11:31; 1 Corinthians 1:30). He is the very treasure of "wisdom and knowledge" (Colossians 2:3). When he taught during his earthly ministry, he used the teaching tool of the sage, the parable, and astounded everyone who heard him. Further, and dramatically, he associated himself with Woman Wisdom (Matthew 11:18-19), and New Testament writers described him using the language of Proverbs 8 (John 1:1-3; Colossians 1:15-17).

In Romans 8:20 Paul talks about how "all creation was subjected to God's curse" (NLT). The Greek word translated "God's curse" (NLT) or "frustration" (NIV) is the equivalent to the Hebrew word translated "meaningless" in the book of Ecclesiastes. Paul is most directly commenting on Genesis 3 and how, due to human sin, God punished Adam, Eve and the serpent in a way that affected the whole cosmos. Qohelet, the Teacher, could only see meaninglessness in the world as he observed it apart from God's revelation ("under the sun"). But Paul in Philippians 2:6-11 describes how Jesus chose to subject himself to the fallen world and even experienced death in order to free us from the meaningless of the fallen world.

1. Why does Paul say that God subjected the world to frustration "with eager hope" (Romans 8:20 NLT)?

While God never tells Job why he suffered, thus shrouding the question with mystery, his ultimate answer to human suffering is Jesus, who is God himself, who suffers on our behalf (see 1 Peter 2:21-25).

2. What does 1 Peter 2:21-25 tell us about God's ultimate response to our suffering?

The Song of Songs is about human love and is not an allegory of our relationship with God. However, that said, the Bible frequently refers to our relationship with God as a marriage. We are God's wife. In the New Testament, Paul describes our relationship with Jesus to be like a marriage (Ephesians 5:21-33). The more we learn about this most intimate of human relationships, the more we learn about God.

3. What does the marriage metaphor of our relationship with God teach us about God and our relationship with him?

The Ancient Story and Our Story

According to the preface to the book of Proverbs, the purpose of that book (and indeed of all biblical wisdom) is "to teach people wisdom" (Proverbs 1:2 NLT). We have observed that wisdom begins with a proper attitude toward God, which encourages us to listen to God's teaching about life and how to live it. The partial list of topics covered by Proverbs includes anger, the appropriate expression of emotions and words, business ethics, family relationships, how to relate to neighbors and friends, planning for the future, protecting the socially vulnerable, and wealth and poverty. Just listing these practical topics demonstrates how relevant a study of the book of Proverbs can be for our lives today. The book also encourages us to observe life to see how it works and learn from our mistakes. In this way, we not only come to learn the proverbs but to know to apply them at the right time. While not making promises or giving guarantees, following the instructions of the book is the best route to desired consequences.

However, the temptation is strong to turn the rewards of wisdom into promises. All one has to do is turn on the television set on Sunday morning to hear what has come to be known as "the prosperity gospel." If you suffer financially or are ill, we hear from certain teachers, it must be the result of a lack of faith. The book of Job is a quick remedy to that false understanding of biblical teaching. Job was "blameless and upright" (Job 1:1), yet he suffered horribly. The book of Job reminds us today that the reasons for our suffering are often hidden from us. Even so, we should trust God who is all-powerful and wise.

Ecclesiastes may be one of the most relevant books in the Bible. After all, we all wonder about the meaning or purpose of life. Ecclesiastes is there to remind us that there is only one sure ground of meaning in life, and that is God. If we try to make money, work or anything else the main purpose of our lives, it will let us down.

Finally, the Song of Songs is a beautiful reminder that sex is a gift from God as it celebrates the physical intimacy between a man and his wife. The Song also points out that such intimacy is not easily won.

LOOKING AHEAD

The four wisdom books contain profound and practical advice for how to approach life. They are deeply theological and point us toward God, who is the source of all wisdom. Next, we turn to the Divided Monarchy of ancient Israel.

Going Deeper

Bartholomew, Craig G., and Ryan P. O'Dowd. *Old Testament Wisdom Literature: A Theological Introduction*. Downers Grove, IL: IVP Academic, 2011.

Longman, Tremper, III. *How to Read Proverbs*. Downers Grove, IL: InterVarsity Press, 2002.

15 / Divided Monarchy

LOOKING AHEAD

MEMORY VERSE: 1 Kings 11:9-13
BIBLE STUDY: 1 Kings 12–13; 15:1-8; 21; 2 Kings 17:5-23; 22:1–23:30; 24:8-20
READING: The Road to Judgment

 ## Bible Study Guide

After reading 1 Kings 12–13; 15:1-8; 21; 2 Kings 17:5-23; 22:1–23:30; 24:8-20, spend some time reflecting on these passages with the following questions in mind before looking at the Reading. (For the whole story read 1 Kings 12–2 Kings 25; 1 Chronicles 10–2 Chronicles 36.)

1. According to 1 Kings 12:1-24 how did Rehoboam, the son of Solomon, lose the support of the northern tribes?

2. Why does Jeroboam, the first king of the northern kingdom (Israel), build golden calf shrines at Dan and Bethel (1 Kings 12:25-33)?

What do the shrines remind you of from Israel's past?

3. What message does the unnamed "man of God" bring to Jeroboam in 1 Kings 13?

What lesson is the reader of 1 Kings 13 to learn from the story about the "man of God" who disobeys God's command not to eat until he returned to Judah?

4. According to 2 Kings 17:5-23 why was the northern kingdom defeated by Assyria?

5. What kind of king was Josiah (2 Kings 22:1–23:30)?

6. According to 2 Kings 24:8-20, how did the southern kingdom of Judah come to its end?

👓 Reading: The Road to Judgment

At the end of our study of the United Monarchy, we saw that King Solomon had departed from the exclusive worship of the Lord. Upon his death (931 B.C.), his son Rehoboam (931–911 B.C.) attempted to assume the throne of Israel, but he was unsuccessful (1 Kings 12). He seems to have been automatically accepted by his home tribe of Judah, but when he traveled north to the city of Shechem in order to receive the ratification of the northern tribes, he ran into resistance. The northern tribes were upset with Solomon because he imposed harsh labor conditions on them; he treated them like Canaanites rather than like fellow Israelites. Rather than listening to his experienced advisers, who told him to soften his approach to the north, Rehoboam heeded the advice of his contemporaries who told him to be harsh on the north. The result was predictable. They rejected Rehoboam as their king and elected Jeroboam, a man we saw in study 12 who had served in Solomon's administration, but then fled to Egypt to seek political asylum after he had a falling out with the king.

The book of Kings then shifts attention to the first years of the northern kingdom under their new king Jeroboam. The northern king faced an immediate problem. The temple was in Jerusalem, located in the south. He knew that Israelites were expected to go to the temple during the three great annual festivals (Passover, Pentecost, Booths). To circumvent this he had two altars constructed at the far north (Dan) and the far south (Bethel) of his kingdom. He erected two golden calves that would be the focus of worship. By creating these alternate worship sites, he not only introduced idol worship as normative in the north, but he also violated the law of centralization (Deuteronomy 12) in which God insisted that sacrificial worship only take place at the one place that God chose. The book of Kings records that every single successive king of the north would continue this abominable practice, thus leading to the ultimate judgment of the northern kingdom.

First Kings 13 also records the first of a number of times when a northern king rejects the message of God as delivered through a prophet. Here an unnamed prophet delivers an oracle announcing the future destruction of the altar in Bethel, a demand that Jeroboam quickly rejects. God's displeasure with Jeroboam is displayed in 1 Kings 14 when the prophet Ahijah tells Jeroboam's wife that their son Abijah would not recover from an illness. He also delivered an oracle against the kings who would descend from Jeroboam: "Since you have turned your back on me, I will bring disaster on your dynasty" (1 Kings 14:9-10 NLT).

While not immediately destroyed, Jeroboam's son Nadab (907–906 B.C.) had a very short reign and was assassinated by

Baasha, a man from the tribe of Issachar who proclaimed himself king (1 Kings 15:25-30). The fact that this assassination happened during a siege of the Philistine city of Gibbethon shows that Israel's borders were shrinking, and thus Israel was descending from the height of its power during the period of Solomon. Baasha himself continued the evil policies of his predecessors and was in continual war with his Judean counterpart. Eventually, Baasha was assassinated by Zimri, who only lasted seven days before he was assassinated by Omri. Omri succeeded in establishing stability in the northern empire, but before considering the dynasty of Omri, we turn back to events in the southern kingdom after Rehoboam.

Rehoboam himself ruled for seventeen years, a time during which "Judah did evil in the eyes of the LORD" (1 Kings 14:22), the worst of this evil having to do with idolatry. There was constant war between the north and the south, and we even learn that Shishak the king of Egypt raided Jerusalem and plundered the temple. Rehoboam was followed by his son Abijah, who also was evil and ruled for three years (1 Kings 15:1-8), and then came Abijah's son Asa, who ruled for forty-one years (908–867 B.C.). Asa was different than his father and grandfather because he "did what was right in the eyes of the LORD, as his father David had done" (1 Kings 15:11); most notably he purified the worship of God. Asa is the first of a handful of kings of Judah who were commended for their faithfulness. All the kings of the

northern empire are evaluated negatively.

The ascension of Omri to the throne of Israel, the northern empire, ushers in a new phase in both kingdoms. The biblical text devotes little space to Omri (1 Kings 16:21-28), but extrabiblical sources indicate that he was a powerful ruler who even extended the boundaries of his kingdom. He also established one of the longer-lasting dynasties of the north.

We know a lot more about his son, Ahab (871–852 B.C.), not because Ahab was more powerful than his father but because Ahab became a conduit for the worship of Baal in Israel. Indeed, because of the religious conflict that develops between Ahab and his sons (Ahaziah and Jehoram), who represent Baal, and God's representatives, the prophets Elijah and Elisha, a considerable section of the story of the divine monarchy is devoted to his reign and the rest of his dynasty (1 Kings 16:29–2 Kings 8:24).

The trouble began in earnest when Ahab married the daughter of the priest-king of neighboring Sidon, the notorious Jezebel. She was fervent in her devotion to the god Baal, and the religion spread like wildfire through Israel. Baal was a storm god, thought to be the force behind the rains that brought fertility in the land. Thus, God first sent Elijah to confront the situation by announcing, "As the LORD, the God of Israel, lives, whom I serve, there will be neither dew nor rain in the next few years except at my word" (1 Kings 17:1). In other words, if the king and the people turn to Baal and expect rain, God will give them drought.

Space does not permit a thorough look at the conflict that develops between God and Baal, or Ahab and his sons and Elijah and Elisha. We will content ourselves with one dramatic example, the confrontation on Mount Carmel (1 Kings 18). Events lead to a contest between Elijah, the lone prophet representing the true God, and the many prophets of Baal. The question is, which God can light the altar fire on top of the mountain? In other words, God is taking on Baal in the area of his specialty. As a storm god, after all, he throws fire from heaven (lightning). To make a long story short, since Baal is not God, his many prophets mourn his absence, while Elijah calls for water to be poured on the altar wood. Even so, the true God lights the fire, and the false prophets are killed.

Though Elijah is victorious on this occasion, Jezebel is more determined then ever, and her husband Ahab as well as his immediate successors (Ahaziah and Jehoram) continue the pro-Baal policies that she instigated. Elijah and his successor Elisha continue to resist their efforts on behalf of God, performing many miracles that show that God is real and superior to anything that Baal represents. The conflict continues until God calls Jehu to bring an end to the dynasty of Omri.

Before we turn our attention to the significant role of Jehu, I need to say a word about Judah in the south during the period of the Omride dynasty in the north. Jehoshaphat the son of Asa (867–846 B.C.) became the king of Judah in the fourth year of Ahab and "was . . . at peace with the

king of Israel" (1 Kings 22:44). From the time of the split, Judah and Israel were at war, and now there was peace. While the circumstances that led to this peace are cloudy, it appears that Jehoshaphat was the lesser partner in the relationship as we look at the way he interacts with Ahab in the war of Ramoth Gilead (1 Kings 22). Even though he consorted with Ahab and his idolatrous children who succeeded him, Jehoshaphat is presented as a godly man, though with some faults. Jehoshaphat's son and grandson (Ahaziah and Jehoram [similarly named to the kings in the north]) followed him as king but are evil.

We now come to the story of Jehu, whose actions make a big impression on both Israel and Judah. Jehu was a general that God used to push back the influence of Baal worship in Israel, though he may have gone too far in his zeal, and then finally succumbed himself to the lure of false religion. Elisha, Elijah's successor, sent an emissary to Jehu when he was the commander of the forces of Israel, who were besieging the town of Ramoth Gilead. This man anointed Jehu to be the next king of Israel (842–814 B.C.). In the next episode (2 Kings 9:14-29), he furiously rides his chariot toward the king of the north, Jehoram (also known by the shorter name Joram). He kills not only Jehoram but also the king of the south, Ahaziah. He then encounters Jezebel, who mocks him, just before he has two of her servants throw her out of the window. He continues his purge by having the seventy sons of Ahab killed. He then tricks all the worshipers of Baal to gather together in the temple of Baal, which he set on fire. God had commissioned him to bring Omri's dynasty to an end because of the depravities of Ahab, but in his zeal Jehu far exceeded that demand. Thus, God both blesses him with a dynasty that lasts for four generations, but Jehu also "refused to turn from the sins that Jeroboam had led Israel to commit" (2 Kings 10:31 NLT).

In the south (Judah), the death of Ahaziah allowed his mother, Athaliah, to seize the throne (842–836 B.C.). Fortunately, quick thinking led to the rescue of Ahaziah's infant son Joash. A few years later, under the capable guidance of the priest Jehoiada, Joash was able to forcibly take the throne (836–798 B.C.). Joash, again under Jehoiada's guidance, purified the temple (which had been polluted with the presence of idols since the last purification at the time of Asa). But Joash himself did not end well. Under military pressure from the king of Aram in the north, he gave him all the treasures of the temple in order to get peace. At the end Joash's own officers assassinated him (2 Kings 12:17-21). Second Chronicles 24 tells us Joash began to worship other gods toward the end of his life, after the death of Jehoiada.

In the north, after Jehu, four of his descendants followed him on the throne, all of them noted for continuing the idolatrous practices of their predecessors. The one king of note in this dynasty is Jeroboam II, only because his kingdom (and the kingdom of Judah under Uzziah) expanded to near unprecedented boundaries. This expansion was due to the relative weakness of Assyria and Egypt, the superpowers of the day.

However, Assyria's weakness was short-lived. When the energetic Tiglath-pileser III (744–727 B.C.) took the throne, he set out to enlarge his empire based in northern Mesopotamia (where present-day Iraq is located). Encouraged by the Judean king Ahaz (733–727 B.C.), the Assyrian attacked Syria and weakened the northern part of Israel. This assault was just the beginning of the end for Israel because God was going to use Assyria to judge Israel for its longstanding neglect of God and its worship of false gods. Jehu's dynasty came to an abrupt end with the assassination of Zechariah in 747 B.C., and the next twenty-five years saw short-lived kings, one killed after another. Finally, under the Assyrian kings Shalmaneser V and Sargon II, Israel was defeated and exiled (722 B.C.). Foreign people were brought into the area, and they intermarried with the people who remained behind. The ten northern tribes were no more, and the children of the mixed marriages would be known as Samaritans.

After the fall of the northern kingdom of Israel, only Judah was left as an independent nation-state. While the descendants of David still ruled Judah, they were vassals of Assyria, paying them an annual tribute. Hezekiah was king in the south (727–698 B.C.) at the time of the defeat of Israel. Considerable attention is given to Hezekiah in the account in Kings (2 Kings 18–20; see also 2 Chronicles 29–32 and Isaiah 36–39). He was not perfect, but he was one of the most faithful kings during the period of the Divided Monarchy, being careful to keep the temple free of idols and getting rid of local shrines. During his reign he was threatened by an invasion from Sennacherib, king of Assyria (Micah 1–2 refers to this as well), but encouraged by the prophet Isaiah, he did not submit to this foreign king, and the Assyrians eventually withdrew after "the angel of the LORD went out and put to death a hundred and eighty-five thousand in the Assyrian camp" (2 Kings 19:35).

If Hezekiah was one of the best kings of this time period, his son Manasseh (698–642 B.C.), who succeeded him, was one of the worst, if not the worst (2 Kings 21). Becoming king when he was twelve, he ruled for fifty-five years. Kings emphasizes his evil by describing how he put pagan altars in the temple and put up altars for Baal. He "sacrificed his own son in the fire, practicing divination, sought omens, and consulted mediums and spiritists. He did much evil in the eyes of the LORD, arousing his anger" (2 Kings 21:6). Interestingly, Chronicles, but not Kings, tells us that Manasseh repented at the end of his life (on why Kings would withhold this information see later on in Kings and Chronicles). Even so, his evil was such that it virtually assured that judgment was coming on the land, and this despite the righteous reign of his grandson Josiah (see 2 Kings 24:3).

After a brief reign by Manasseh's son Amon (641–640 B.C.), Amon's son Josiah became king at the age of eight and ruled for thirty-one years (640–609 B.C.). In a summarizing statement, the author of Kings states, "he did what was right in the eyes of the LORD and followed completely the ways of his father David, not turning aside to the right or to the left" (2 Kings 22:2). He cleansed the temple, and while doing so discovered the Book of the Law, which apparently had been hidden away by the idolatrous kings who preceded him (2 Kings 22:8-20). This law inspired him to even more religious reforms, including the destruction of the altar to the golden calf in Bethel that Jeroboam I constructed at the beginning of the Divided Monarchy (2 Kings 23:15-20).

During his reign, events in the broader ancient Near East were heating up. In 626 B.C. Babylon, which was a vassal state of Assyria, revolted. In 612 B.C. the Babylonians took the capital city Nineveh (as prophesied by the prophet Nahum). The remnants of the Assyrians relocated to northern Syria, and in 609 B.C. Necho, the pharaoh of Egypt, mobilized his troops to go up to Carchemish in order to support the Assyrians against the Babylonians, whom they saw as the greater threat. As Necho went north, Josiah attacked him at Megiddo. Josiah had no love for the Assyrians, to whom he was paying tribute. However, he was not only unsuccessful in his attempt to stop him, but Josiah also died in the attempt, bringing an end to the last glimmer of hope for a righteous people of God.

The kings who succeeded Josiah included, in order, two sons (Jehoahaz, Jehoiakim), a grandson (Jehoiachin) and a third son (Zedekiah). We not only learn about this period of time from the historical books but also from the accounts of the prophets who confronted them (most notably Jeremiah and Ezekiel). The bottom line was that these kings refused to listen to God and obey the law, and they did not respond to the warnings of the prophets.

The Babylonians went on to defeat the coalition of Assyrians and Egyptians at Carchemish in 609 B.C. In the first chapter of the book of Daniel (see study 16), we hear about a preliminary siege of Jerusalem by the new Babylonian king Nebuchadnezzar (605 B.C.). At this point Judah becomes a vassal of Babylon. The prophets inform the Judean kings and the people that this situation is a result of their sin.

They needed to repent and submit to the Babylonians. Jehoiakim does not listen, and in 597 B.C. he rebels against Babylon, only to have the city besieged, and once it fell, Jehoiachin, Jehoiakim's son who was on the throne, was carried off into exile along with many leading citizens, including a young priest and prophet Ezekiel. Nebuchadnezzar then placed Zedekiah on the throne, but in 587 B.C. he made the fateful decision to rebel against Babylon. When Nebuchadnezzar came this time, he was ready to take the next step and destroy Jerusalem and incorporate Judah as a province within his vast empire. Thus, in 587 B.C. Judah met the same fate as Israel did in 722 B.C. However, as study 17 will show, unlike Israel, Judah would survive the exile.

Reading Study Guide

1. Why did Israel divide into two kingdoms, the northern kingdom of Israel and the southern kingdom of Judah?

2. Why did Jeroboam build the calf shrines in Dan and Bethel?

   What was the long-term significance of this for the history of the northern kingdom?

   What happened to these shrines?

3. What is the significance of King Omri?

4. What is the significance of Elijah and Elisha during this period?

5. What role did the god Baal play during this period of time?

6. How did God and his prophets confront the problem of the worship of Baal among the people of God?

7. What role did Jehu play in the war against Baal? How did he end his life?

8. From a theological perspective, why did the southern kingdom last longer than the northern kingdom?

9. Were there any godly kings who ruled the northern kingdom? The southern kingdom?

10. How did God use foreign nations like Assyria and Babylon for his purposes?

11. Evaluate the reigns of Hezekiah and Josiah, and compare them with the reign of Manasseh.

Anticipating the New Testament

As the name of the books imply (1–2 Kings), they follow the development of kingship among God's people. During the period of Judges, with its chaotic society and horrible relationship with God, the faithful yearned for a strong king to lead them to better times. After a rocky start with Saul, David, though not perfect, was the model of kingship, uniting Israel and fervent in his devotion to God. For this reason God entered into a covenant relationship with him, promising that he would have a son on the throne forever.

That same covenant also promised that if his sons were disobedient, then God would "punish him with a rod wielded by men, with floggings inflicted by human hands" (2 Samuel 7:14). Beginning with the latter part of Solomon's reign, Israel's and Judah's kings show themselves to be imperfect leaders. All twenty northern kings and most of the twenty southern kings practice some form of idolatry. Indeed, after David, only Hezekiah and Josiah are given unqualified praise.

Thus, the dark history of kingship in Israel demonstrates that this human institution is not the final answer to the problems of God's people and humankind in general. In study 12, we have seen that Jesus Christ is the ultimate fulfillment of the promise of an anointed king, a Messiah. However, before things get better, they get far worse.

1. What is the significance of Jesus being called the Christ (the Greek equivalent of Messiah)?

2. How is Jesus the perfect Messiah compared to the imperfect messiahs who were the sons of David who ruled in Jerusalem during the Old Testament period?

⬤ The Ancient Story and Our Story

The biblical presentation of the period of the Divided Monarchy is filled with many names (between Israel and Judah there were forty kings), a number of which I cited in the essay. It is hard to remember the names of these kings, and, while trying to follow this complicated history, we should not lose sight of the important themes that arise out of the biblical account of this time period that have bearing on our lives today.

The main lesson that we should learn is that sin, particularly the sin of worshiping false gods, is dangerous and leads to horrible consequences. The kingdoms of Israel and Judah struggled through their histories and ultimately suffered great loss (see study 16) because of their sin. Granted, consequences did not come immediately, and this delay probably gave some people the idea that God would not punish sin. But judgment eventually did come.

It is true that not every sin is punished in this life, and not every act of kindness is rewarded in this life, as we saw in the message of the book of Job (and to a lesser extent Ecclesiastes; see study 14). However, we also know that this life is not the end of the story. The message of the New Testament is that sure judgment awaits those who turn away from following the true God and instead worship false gods.

The major sin of this period was the worship of false gods, thus breaking the first of the Ten Commandments. Modern people err if they think they are not prone to idol worship today. Certainly, not many, at least in the modern West, bow down to idols that represent divine beings. However, a false god is anything except the true God that is the most important thing in one's life. With this understanding we can see how money, work, pleasure, relationships or any thing or person can become a "god" that replaces the true God, and the story of the Divided Monarchy warns us against such beliefs, attitudes and behaviors.

Looking Ahead

The Divided Kingdom comes to an end with the destruction of Jerusalem and the removal of the last Davidic king from the throne. The next and final phase of Old Testament history concerns the period of the exile and the restoration that follows. However, before addressing that period of time, we turn our attention to the prophets whom God used to try to avoid the judgment of the exile.

Going Deeper

Konkel, August H. *1 & 2 Kings*. NIV Application Commentary. Grand Rapids: Zondervan, 2006.

16 / Prophets

MEMORY VERSE: Amos 3:7
BIBLE STUDY: Jeremiah 1:1-10; 10–11; 13:1-14; 20:7-18; 31; Daniel 1; 7
READING: God's Covenant Lawyers and Apocalyptic Visionaries

 Bible Study Guide

After reading Jeremiah 1:1-10; 10–11; 13:1-14; 20:7-18; 31; Daniel 1; 7, spend some time reflecting on these passages with the following questions in mind before looking at the Reading. (For maximum benefit read Isaiah, Jeremiah, Ezekiel, Daniel, Hosea, Joel, Amos, Obadiah, Jonah, Micah, Nahum, Habakkuk, Zephaniah, Haggai, Zechariah and Malachi in their entirety.)

1. Jeremiah 1:1-10 records Jeremiah's prophetic call. What was God calling Jeremiah to do?

2. Jeremiah 10–11 records two of Jeremiah's judgment oracles. In your own words, what was Jeremiah telling the people of Judah?

3. In Jeremiah 13:1-14, we hear God tell Jeremiah to wear and not wash his linen loincloth, and then to hide it in a cleft of a rock near the Euphrates River. What message was God trying to communicate through Jeremiah's actions?

4. In Jeremiah 20:7-18 we see Jeremiah grow angry with God but also express confidence in God. Why is he so conflicted?

5. What are the features of the new covenant according to Jeremiah 31:31-34?

6. Why would Nebuchadnezzar take sacred objects from the temple and also some of the "young men of Judah's royal family" (Daniel 1:1-4)?

7. What motivates the Babylonians to change Daniel and his three friends' names?

8. Why did the four Hebrew boys not want to eat the food and drink the wine that King Nebuchadnezzar supplied?

9. In Daniel 7, what do the beasts that arise out of the sea represent?

10. What is the climax of the vision that Daniel has, according to Daniel 7, and what effect would the vision have on people of faith?

⊙ Reading: God's Covenant Lawyers and Apocalyptic Visionaries

In this section, we will study God's prophets and his apocalyptic visionaries. The two are closely connected in that God gives both divinely inspired insight into the future, but there are differences as well, as we will see by comparing Jeremiah, a prophet, with Daniel, an apocalyptic visionary.

Since I cannot cover all the prophets in this short essay, I will take a look at Jeremiah. While each prophet displays his unique personality, style and historical situation, we will focus in on Jeremiah in a way that will help us interpret the other prophets as well.

When most people think about the Old Testament prophets, they first identify them as those whom God uses to reveal the future to his people. Of course, they do, but it is important to realize that the prophets talk about the future in order to evoke a present response from their contemporaries. In other words, the prophets do not talk about the future primarily for the benefit of future readers who live after the time the prophecies are fulfilled, but rather to get their hearers to change their behavior.

Indeed, it is helpful to think of the Old Testament prophets as lawyers, covenant lawyers. In our study on law (study 8), I talked briefly about the covenant between God and Israel. A covenant is like a treaty between a great king and his subjects. The great king takes care of his people, and the people must obey the laws of the king in order to get rewarded and avoid punishment. The book of Deuteronomy is structured like a covenant-treaty with its long legal section (Deuteronomy 4–26) followed by curses and blessings (Deuteronomy 27–28). When Israel disobeys God's law, they become subject to God's judgment. However, before God executes the judgment, he sends his prophets in order to bring a case against Israel and accuse them of lawbreaking with the hope that they will repent and restore their relationship with God. The prophets tell the people about the future, specifically the coming judgment if they don't repent.

We will now turn to the prophet Jeremiah as an illustration of a prophet. Like most prophetic books, Jeremiah opens with a superscription (Jeremiah 1:1-3) that sets the following prophecies in a historical context. Since prophets speak directly to their contemporaries, it is important for modern readers to know something about the historical setting of the prophet.

Jeremiah's superscription situates his prophecies in the period leading up to the destruction of Jerusalem. God calls him as a prophet in the thirteenth year of good king Josiah, the year Babylon began its imperialistic expansion in the Near East (626 B.C.; see the end of the essay on the Divided Monarchy [study 15] for more detail on this time period), and he continues through the eighteenth year of Zedekiah, the year that Jerusalem fell to the Babylonians (587 B.C.). While not every speech is dated in the book of Jeremiah, we can now see that Jeremiah is preaching in a very tumultuous time. He is telling Judah and its kings that the rising Babylonian threat is a sign of God's judgment for their sins, and that they had better repent or their nation will be overwhelmed.

Besides a superscription, many prophets also include an account of their prophetic call, the time that God commissioned them for their task. Perhaps the most famous call is the encounter between God and Moses at the burning bush (Exodus 3). Jeremiah writes about his call in Jeremiah 1:4-10. Like Moses, Jeremiah tries to resist God's call, but God assures the prophet of his presence. We should further notice the double-edged nature of God's commission (v. 10). It has a negative side, judgment, as well as a positive side, restoration. As we look at Jeremiah's sermons and actions that follow, we will see that, while his message is predominantly one of judgment, he also delivers the hope of restoration.

For samples of Jeremiah's message of judgment, we turn first to chapter 11 and then to chapter 10. In Jeremiah 11 we see Jeremiah getting right to the heart of the matter by saying, "Listen to the terms of this covenant and tell them to the people of Judah and to those who live in Jerusalem" (v. 2). He goes on to say, "Cursed is the one who does not obey the terms of my covenant" (v. 3). Jeremiah 10 is another oracle that specifies what we come to realize is the main charge against God's people, the worship of false gods rather than the true God. While this is the main accusation against Judah, other oracles will also name their deceit, adultery, theft, sabbath breaking and so on. In short, they are breaking all of the Ten Commandments and thus deserve punishment.

Jeremiah 13 illustrates that Jeremiah did more than preach his message of the need for repentance. He also did actions that supported his basic message. Here God tells him to put on a linen loincloth (the equivalent of what we know as underwear) but not wash it. Eventually God tells him to take this dirty underwear and hide it in a crevice. Later he retrieves this garment, and of course it is "ruined and completely useless" (v. 7). He takes this loincloth back to Jerusalem along with the message that because of their sin the people of Judah were like that loincloth. Of course, the hope was that they would hear this message and avoid the horrible fate that was about to befall them.

However, neither king nor people responded favorably to God's message as given through Jeremiah. They hated him and persecuted him. Jeremiah struggled with the reaction to his message, even growing angry with God for putting him in this position (Jeremiah 20:7-18). Even so, he persisted in obedience to God in spite of the pain that it caused him. Since he was God's messenger, the people's ill treatment of Jeremiah revealed their true heart attitude toward God.

Accordingly, God acted on his warnings. The people listened to false prophets who told them that there was no problem, and rejected the message of the true prophet who told them to repent (Jeremiah 27–28). Thus, God eventually executed his judgment against them by allowing the Babylonians to defeat them and exile their leading citizens (Jeremiah 39; 52).

Thus Jeremiah, like all the other prophets, comes initially and mainly with a message of judgment. However, as mentioned earlier, there was a second important component of his message, one of hope and restoration. As it turned out, since the people did not repent, the restoration would come after the judgment, but it would eventually be a magnificent restoration. The messages of hope are collected together and found in chapters 30–33, a section of Jeremiah often called the Book of Compassion (or Comfort).

The most famous oracle (for reasons to be explained later in "Anticipating the New Testament") is the promise of a new covenant:

> "The days are coming," declares the LORD,
>> "when I will make a new covenant
> with the people of Israel
>> and the people of Judah.
> It will not be like the covenant
>> I made with their ancestors
> when I took them by the hand
>> to lead them out of Egypt,
> because they broke my covenant,
>> though I was a husband to them,"
>>> declares the LORD.

> "This is the covenant I will make
>> with the people of Israel
> after that time," declares the LORD.
> "I will put my law in their minds
>> and write it on their hearts.
> I will be their God,
>> and they will be my people.
> No longer will they teach their neighbor,
>> or say to one another, 'Know the LORD,'
> because they will all know me,
>> from the least of them to the greatest,"
>>> declares the LORD.
> "For I will forgive their wickedness
>> and will remember their sins no more." (Jeremiah 31:31-34)

The bottom line is that God's judgment is not the end of the story for God's people. They will experience restoration after judgment (see study 17). The promise that God will bless his people and "all peoples on earth" (Genesis 12:1-3) will continue.

While prophets like Jeremiah bring a vision of the future to God's people with the hope that they will repent and avoid the consequences of their sin, an apocalyptic visionary like Daniel announces the sure judgment of those who wickedly oppress God's people, thus bringing a message of hope to the latter. Prophets speak to God's people when they are sinning, while visionaries speak to God's people when they need hope in the midst of oppression.

Daniel lived during a time of oppression. The opening chapter (Daniel 1:1-2) narrates the first time that Babylon reduces Judah to the status of a vassal country (605 B.C.), and Daniel himself lives into the time period when the Persians replace Babylon as an oppressive presence in Judah, and he also foresees the time that the Greeks will replace the Persians and the Romans will replace the Greeks. Again, Daniel speaks to the faithful with an important message: In spite of present circumstances, God is in control and he will have the final victory.

The book of Daniel is made up of six stories (chaps. 1–6) and four visions (chaps. 7–12), and each story and vision illustrates this main theme. For our purposes, we will focus on one story (chap. 1, with a brief look at chap. 2) and one vision (chap. 7).

As mentioned earlier, Daniel begins with an account of Nebuchadnezzar's first intrusion into the affairs of the kingdom of Judah, who is ruled at this time by King Jehoiakim. It is his third year of rule (605 B.C.), and Nebuchadnezzar successfully makes Jehoiakim submit to his rule as indicated by two acts that are typical to the situation according to ancient Near Eastern custom. First, Jehoiakim turns over objects from the temple to Nebuchadnezzar. In most cases the idol of a country's chief god was given over and placed in Babylon's temple, but since Israel did not have idols, the sacred objects (cups, dishes, forks, etc.) were the next best thing. Second, the Babylonians took hostages from among the noble classes; in this case we hear about Daniel and his three friends.

The purpose behind taking these hostages would be to train them in Babylonian ways in order to shift their loyalties away from their own nation and God, in this case Yahweh, and toward Babylon and its gods. They would then be made to serve the interests of the expanding Babylonian Empire.

Events on the ground made it look like Nebuchadnezzar and Babylon were in control, but the biblical text reveals otherwise. In Daniel 1:2 we read, "The Lord delivered Jehoiakim king of Judah into his [Nebuchadnezzar's] hand." In other words, the only reason why Nebuchadnezzar succeeded in taking Jerusalem was because God permitted it. God is in control and is letting these things happen for his own purposes.

Now the scene shifts to the Babylonian royal court, where Nebuchadnezzar attempts to "Babylonianize" Daniel and the three friends. It is interesting to observe the Babylonian king's strategy to do so and how Daniel and his three friends resist being transformed into successful Babylonian subjects. In other words, in spite of the effort, they remain completely loyal to Yahweh, but it is interesting to see where they draw the line.

For one thing, as part of the program of indoctrination, the Babylonians change their names. Their good Hebrew names that praise the Lord are changed to Babylonian names that praise the Babylonian gods. We will take the name Daniel as an example. Daniel means "God is my judge," and it is changed to Belteshazzar, which means "the divine lady protects the king." Even more significantly, the four Hebrew men are required to attend Nebuchadnezzar's school, where they were to show "aptitude for every kind of learning" and be "well informed, quick to understand" so they are "qualified to serve in the king's palace." Thus they are to be trained "in the language and literature of Babylon" in order to become wise men (Daniel 1:4).

In short, they are to be subjected to an education that is toxic to their faith. Through archaeological discovery, we know the curriculum for the education of Babylonian wise men. It would include learning the Akkadian language and reading the myths of the false religion of Babylon. In addition, there would be a heavy dose of divination training. They would be able to tell the future by astrology and reading the livers of sheep, and they would also learn how to interpret the significance of dreams. The latter will be important for our understanding of Daniel 2, so I should point out that in Babylon dreams were interpreted by reference to commentaries. The dreamer would tell the wise man his dream, and then the wise man would go to his dream commentaries to learn the significance of the different elements of his dream.

While this curriculum would be hostile to their faith, the Hebrew men went to the school and even graduated at the top of their class! They had another requirement as well. The Babylonians were not just interested in their minds; they were also interested in their bodies. Thus Nebuchadnezzar ordered his chief of staff, Ashpenaz, to serve them "food and wine given to them by the king" (Daniel 1:8 NLT). What

was their intention? They wanted these men to look like wise men. From ancient art, we know that Babylonian wise men were chubby, and for that reason Ashpenaz did not allow Daniel and his friends to substitute vegetables and water for fear that they become "pale and thin compared to the other youths" (Daniel 1:10 NLT).

Though Ashpenaz would not help them avoid eating the food from the king, Daniel found a way to eat only vegetables and water by convincing the person who delivered it to them. Why don't the four men want to eat the king's food? The text does not say directly, but it strongly suggests that their avoidance of the Babylonian food was only temporary during the time of the their training (see Daniel 10:2-3, which implies that Daniel had been eating "choice food . . . meat" and drinking "wine" later in life). Thus, it does not seem likely, as many believe, that Daniel is intent on only eating foods that are ritually clean (Leviticus 11).

Daniel and the three friends are giving God room to work. In other words, Nebuchadnezzar is trying to turn these men into paragons of Babylonian wisdom teachers by their education and diet. And at the end of the chapter when they are pronounced the best in their class, Nebuchadnezzar would take the credit. However, the four men (and those of us who read it today) know that they have not been eating the food from the king's table but rather were eating a diet that should have left them thin and pale. Even so, because of God they were the most robust of all. Nebuchadnezzar is not in control—God is. In other words, they were in the physical shape desired by Nebuchadnezzar because of God, not because of the food provided by the king.

But, of course, at the end of Daniel 1, it does appear that their wisdom is the result of their Babylonian training. A brief look at chapter 2 changes that impression.

In Daniel 2 Nebuchadnezzar has a disturbing dream. As a result, he wants his wise men to interpret its significance for him. He even wants them to tell him the contents of his dream. As mentioned earlier, this procedure is not typical to ancient Babylonian custom. The custom was for the dreamer to inform the interpreter of the dream, and then the interpreter would consult the dream commentaries. For whatever reasons, Nebuchadnezzar refused to tell them the contents of his dream, and the wise men responded that this was unprecedented and unfair (Daniel 2:10-11). Even so, since they cannot tell him his dream, he then orders that all the wise men in Babylon be killed.

When the commander of the king's guard comes to round up Daniel and the three friends, Daniel requests some time. He then informs the other three, and they pray that God would reveal to them the contents of the dream and its interpretation. God answers their prayers, and Daniel goes to Nebuchadnezzar to give him the information that he wants. Thus, the wisdom of the four men does not derive from the learning they received in the royal court but in God's wisdom, which he chose to reveal to them. Again, Nebuchadnezzar is not in control; God is, and God will have the final victory.

Daniel 7 is the first vision of the second half of the book and will be our example to represent the other four visions and the nature of apocalyptic itself. Indeed, Daniel 1–6 shares its main theme with Daniel 7–12 (in spite of present circumstances, God is in control and will have the victory), but the stories are not really apocalyptic.

Daniel 7 is dated to the first year of King Belshazzar's reign in Babylon. We know him from the book of Daniel as the king who ruled in Babylon at the time Babylon falls to the Persians (see Daniel 5), though other ancient Near Eastern sources indicate that he was ruling with his father Nabonidus, who had earlier been defeated by the Persians on the open battlefield. In any case, this vision comes from very early in Belshazzar's co-regency with his father.

The rest of the chapter details Daniel's vision as well as its interpretation, and here we see the beginnings of the difference between apocalyptic and prophecy. A prophet like Jeremiah would receive a word from God, and then he was commissioned to speak the word to the people with the hope of evoking a positive response from them. With Daniel, as is typical in apocalyptic, he receives a vision he does not understand. That vision is described in verses 2-14. Then an angel, not God, appears to him to interpret the vision (vv. 15-28), and there is no commission to tell the people about it. Indeed, Daniel says that "I kept the matter to myself" (v. 28). Of course, the faithful hear and read about this vision, but the purpose is not to change their minds but rather to reassure them. The vision, as we will see, informs the persecuted faithful that God has things under control and that at the end he will have the victory.

The vision in Daniel 7 starts by describing a disturbing scene (vv. 2-3). The picture is of a shore where the sea has been whipped into a frenzy by the wind. In the ancient Near East and in the Bible, the sea often is a symbol of chaos and even evil. Four beasts arise out of the sea, each more terrifying than the next. The first is a hybrid, part lion, part eagle, part human. To Israelites hybrids were repulsive and terrifying. The second beast is a bear, raised on one leg and chewing on three ribs. The third is also a hybrid, a leopard with four heads and four wings. And the final beast is not like any known beast. We only learn that it has "large iron teeth" (v. 7) and "bronze claws" (v. 19), a kind of robo-beast. It also had ten horns (v. 7), horns being symbols of power in the Old Testament.

The action continues even after the description of the four beasts, because a small horn suddenly emerges from the beast with ten horns, and this horn dislodges three of the other horns. This little horn is described as having "eyes like the eyes of a human being and a mouth that spoke boastfully" (v. 8).

The angel will eventually inform Daniel that these beasts "represent four king-doms that will arise from the earth" (v. 17 NLT). In other words, they stand for evil human nations that oppress God's people. Can we be any more specific? Many think we can be, though there are two main schools of thought. Some believe that the nations represent Babylon, Media, Persia and then Greece, and the little horn stands for a particularly violent persecutor of the Jewish people in the second century B.C. named Antiochus Epiphanes. Others see in these four beasts, Rome followed by the Medo-Persian Empire, then Greece and Rome. The ten horns represent kings or nations that come from the Roman Empire, and the little horn stands for the antichrist at the end of time. A more reasonable interpretation does not press the imagery to come up with specific identifications, but rather understands the imagery to point to the fact that one evil nation will succeed another in dominance until the end of time.

So the end of time and the fall of human evil is the subject of the second part of the vision in vv. 8-14. The scene shifts from the sea, from which horrific animals emerge that represent evil human kingdoms, to a courtroom where human characters who represent God sit in judgment. The one called the "Ancient One" sat down to judge, and into his presence came "one like a son of man, coming with the clouds of heaven" (v. 13). While clear teaching on the three-part nature of the Godhead awaits the New Testament, this description anticipates that. The Ancient One clearly is God, but then only God rides the cloud. As we will see later, the New Testament authors saw this distinction as significant.

The finale of this drama is the utter defeat of the beasts, thus signifying the end of oppression, the end of evil. God will indeed have the victory at the end and "the holy people of the Most High will receive the kingdom and will possess it forever—yes, for ever and ever" (v. 18).

Reading Study Guide

1. Describe the difference between prophecy, as represented by Jeremiah, and apocalyptic, as represented by Daniel.

2. In what way is a prophet like a lawyer?

   What is a prophet's connection to the covenant?

3. What is the main charge that Jeremiah brings against the people of Judah?

   What are the subsidiary charges?

4. In the account of Jeremiah's call to the prophetic ministry, God said he would protect him (Jeremiah 1:8), but Jeremiah got thrown into jail and was often persecuted by his family and fellow citizens. In what way did God protect him?

5. Why didn't the people listen to Jeremiah, and what eventually happened to them?

6. Describe the difference between the old covenant and the new covenant as it is described in Jeremiah 31:31-34.

7. In Daniel 1, how did Daniel as a person of faith respond to being thrown into an environment that was toxic to his faith?

8. Explain in your own words why Daniel and the three friends would not eat the food and wine provided by Nebuchadnezzar.

9. What did the beasts represent in Daniel's vision?

Various suggestions were given in the essay for a more specific identification of the beasts. What is your opinion?

10. In what way would the vision of Daniel 7 encourage someone living in a culture that is toxic to their faith?

Anticipating the New Testament

Deuteronomy 18:15-22 anticipates a line of prophets that will come after the time of Moses and helps Israelites tell the difference between true and false prophets (see also Deuteronomy 13:1-5). Indeed, Jeremiah is one such prophet, and many believe that his hesitation to accept his prophetic task at his call is reminiscent of Moses' reluctance (Exodus 4:10-14). But the New Testament suggests that Deuteronomy 18 has even further significance (see Acts 3:17-26).

1. How does Jesus relate to the promise of future prophets as given in Deuteronomy 18?

Jeremiah 31:31-34 looked to the future and saw that God was going to enter into a new covenant with his people. In Hebrews 7 the author of Hebrews recognizes that through Jesus Christians lived at the time of fulfillment of this promise.

2. How does Jesus relate to the New Covenant promise?

Daniel looked in the future and saw that God would intervene and rescue his people from their oppressive enemies. Daniel 7 pictured "one like the son of man" who would come riding the cloud and doing battle against those enemies. Mark 13:24-26 and Revelation 1:1-8 depict Jesus as coming on the clouds.

3. How does Jesus relate to the "one like the son of man" in Daniel 7?

The Ancient Story and Our Story

We need to pay attention to the message of the prophets today. We are prone to sin. John Calvin called the human mind a "factory of idols." What he meant was that through our thoughts and actions we often place other things or other people in the most important place in our lives. We thus make them gods, but they are false gods. We need to hear the message of the prophets calling us to repentance and back to a healthy relationship with God. And we should remember, in the words of the new covenant (quoted in Hebrews 8:12), that God tells us: "For I will forgive their wickedness, and I will remember their sins no more."

The message of the apocalyptic book of Daniel remains vitally relevant to Christians today. We too need to remember that in spite of present circumstances, God is in control and we will have the victory. While our culture is not as dangerous to our faith as that of ancient Babylon, it is still toxic. We too need wisdom to know how to navigate our lives in a way that does not compromise our faith. Daniel did not have to completely reject Babylonian ways (he went to their school and graduated valedictorian), but he did find a place where he drew a line in the sand. The book of Daniel does not give us a blueprint to follow, but it does call us to be sensitive to and aware of those things that threaten our faith in our society. But most of all Daniel remains relevant in reminding us that God is coming at the end of time. He will eradicate evil, and he will rescue his people so that they "will shine like the brightness of the heavens" (Daniel 12:3).

Looking Ahead

Starting with Moses, the first prophet (though note that Abraham is also called a prophet in Genesis 20:7), we read about prophets throughout Israel's history. They warned about coming judgment and also the restoration that would follow. Study 17 will see that God's judgment eventually comes on his people in the Babylonian destruction of the city of Jerusalem and the exile. We will also see the beginning of the fulfillment of the promises of restoration in the return to Jerusalem after the demise of the Babylonian Empire.

Going Deeper

Dearman, J. Andrew. *Jeremiah, Lamentations*. NIV Application Commentary. Grand Rapids: Zondervan, 2002.

Hays, J. Daniel. *The Message of the Prophets: A Survey of the Prophetic and Apocalyptic Books of the Old Testament*. Grand Rapids: Zondervan, 2010.

Longman, Tremper, III. *Daniel*. NIV Application Commentary. Grand Rapids: Zondervan, 1999.

17 / Exile and Return

LOOKING AHEAD

MEMORY VERSE: Esther 4:14
BIBLE STUDY: Ezekiel 9–11; 2 Kings 25:1-26; Lamentations 2; Ezra 1; 7; Nehemiah 1–2; 13; Esther 9
READING: Divine Hostility and Restoration

 Bible Study Guide

After reading Ezekiel 9–11; 2 Kings 25:1-26; Lamentations 2; Ezra 1; 7; Nehemiah 1–2; 13; Esther 9, spend some time reflecting on these passages with the following questions in mind before looking at the Reading.

1. Read Ezekiel 9–11 and follow the movement of "the glory of God." What is the significance of the movement of God's glory from "above the cherubim" (signifying God's seat in the Holy of Holies [Ezekiel 9:3]) to "the mountain east" of Jerusalem (the Mount of Olives [Ezekiel 11:23])?

2. According to 2 Kings 25, what triggers Nebuchadnezzar's attack on Jerusalem?

3. What does Nebuchadnezzar do to the city, the king, and the city's inhabitants and buildings once he successfully breaches the city walls?

4. King Jehoiachin had been sent into exile at an earlier period of time (see study 15). What is the significance of ending the book of Kings with the report that he has been released from prison in Babylon?

5. Lamentations was written right after the destruction of Jerusalem. Who does the poet of Lamentations 2 think destroyed the city?

How is God characterized in the poem?

6. King Cyrus is the Persian king who defeated Babylon and inherited its empire, including Judah. According to Ezra 1, what is his first act concerning Judah?

7. Who is Ezra, and according to Ezra 7:25-26 what was the mission that the Persian king Artaxerxes gave him?

8. Who is Nehemiah according to Nehemiah 1–2?

What is his mission?

9. Nehemiah 13 ends the book and appears right after a tremendous celebration of the completion of the wall and the reestablishment of the law in Jerusalem (Nehemiah 8–12). How does Nehemiah describe the state of Judah in chapter 13?

10. Describe the feast of Purim (Esther 9). What does it celebrate?

Reading: Divine Hostility and Restoration

The last king of Judah was Zedekiah, a descendant of David, who had been appointed by Nebuchadnezzar of Babylon to replace his nephew Jehoiachin, who was king in Jerusalem after his father Jehoiakim had rebelled against Babylon in 597 B.C. Jehoiachin had been carried off to Babylon in exile along with a number of other leading citizens of Judah. Still, Nebuchadnezzar allowed Judah to have their own monarchy even though he insisted that they remain subservient to him.

For reasons about which we are unsure (but likely because he hoped for support from the Egyptians), Zedekiah chose to rebel against Nebuchadnezzar in the ninth year of his reign. Nebuchadnezzar had now had it with this troublesome vassal nation. He mobilized his army, and they marched the over one-thousand-mile journey to Jerusalem.

Once there, the Babylonians laid siege to the city, and in Zedekiah's eleventh year (587 B.C.) they breached the walls. The siege itself was horrific because after a while "the famine in the city had become so severe that there was no food for the people to eat" (2 Kings 25:3). But once the walls were breached, destruction was unleashed on the city and its inhabitants.

Zedekiah and his sons ran for their lives but were caught by the Babylonians and shipped to Riblah in Syria where the Babylonian army had its staging area. There Nebuchadnezzar commanded that the king's sons be killed in the presence of Zedekiah, and then his eyes were plucked out so the death of his sons would be the last thing he would ever see. After this, Zedekiah was placed in bronze shackles and carted off to Babylon, never to be heard from again.

Back in Babylon the army began a systematic and intentional dismantling of the city. Prominent houses and important buildings, including the palace, were torn down. The defensive wall of the city was destroyed. Most shockingly, the temple was burned down, and the precious metals used in the temple precincts were taken back to Babylon.

The temple, after all, was the symbol of God's presence in Judah. It was God's home on earth (see study 9). When Jeremiah warned Judah and its kings of the coming judgment, he spoke to their presumption that God would not allow the city to be destroyed because it was the location of his house (Jeremiah 9). What they did not consider was that the temple was a symbol, and that God was not restricted to this building. As Solomon said, when the temple was first dedicated back in the tenth century B.C., "But will God really dwell on earth? The heavens, even the highest heaven, cannot contain you. How much less this temple I have built!" (1 Kings 8:27).

But God did make his presence dwell there—until the people's sin grew to the point that judgment was inevitable. At that point God abandoned the temple. The prophet Ezekiel (Ezekiel 9–11) describes how God rose up from his throne in the Holy of Holies and moved to the courtyard where he was met by the cherubim and his heavenly chariot. The last we see him in this section of Scripture is hovering over the Mount of Olives heading east. The next time Judah would see him would be at the head of the Babylonian army attacking Jerusalem!

Not only were the buildings destroyed, but many people were exiled to Babylon. Though we do not get numbers, many people had died in the siege and in the taking of the city. Among those who survived, the leading citizens were taken into exile and transported to Babylon. The text mentions that the poor of the land were permitted to remain in Judah, which was now incorporated as a province of the empire of Babylon. Of course, the number of poor likely outnumbered the upper classes that were taken to Babylon, but the removal of the priests, royal class and merchants would have decimated the society.

We get a sense of the emotional impact of the destruction of Jerusalem and the period of the exile, not so much from the reports we get in 2 Kings 25 (see also 2 Chronicles 36:15-21; Jeremiah 39; 52) but rather from the book of Lamentations. As the name suggests, the book contains five poems that lament the plight of destroyed Jerusalem and beg God to restore their fortunes. The first chapter pictures Jerusalem as a widow who weeps at her desolation, while chapter 3 uses a different personification of the city, a man of affliction who has suffered the punishment of God.

So now the people of God were fragmented. Some were in Babylon and many were in Judah. Nebuchadnezzar had allowed the prophet Jeremiah, who had been preaching surrender to Babylon, to choose whether to go to Babylon or stay in the land. Jeremiah chose the latter. In Jeremiah 40–44 we hear about events in Judah in the years right after the destruction of Jerusalem, and the picture is not pretty.

Nebuchadnezzar had chosen Gedaliah, a Jewish man, to be governor of the new Babylonian province of Yehud. We know that Gedaliah's family was among the minority who had supported Jeremiah's ministry, so his appointment is hopeful. Perhaps the people who remained behind would learn their lesson and grow close to the Lord in worship and obedience again.

Gedaliah was interested in brokering peace between the Babylonians and the remnants of the Judean army who had sought refuge in the caves in the wilderness areas around the city. Thus, when Ishmael, a leader of the insurgents, contacted him and agreed to a peace talk, Gedaliah invited him to his home. But it was all a ruse. When Ishmael arrived at Gedaliah's home, he assassinated him and overran the Babylonian garrison. After this, Ishmael tried to flee to the neighboring kingdom of Ammon but was overtaken by allies of Gedaliah, who killed him.

Ishmael may be dead, but now the people feared Nebuchadnezzar's response. To their credit, they went to Jeremiah and asked him to inquire of God as to what they should do, stay or flee from Nebuchadnezzar's coming wrath.

Ten days later Jeremiah went to the people with God's response. Stay! Everything will be all right. Rather than obeying the Lord, they shouted, "You are lying! The LORD our God has not sent you to say, 'You must not go to Egypt to settle there'" (Jeremiah 43:2). So off to Egypt they went, forcing Jeremiah to go with them, showing they were no better than before the judgment on Jerusalem.

Thus the Diaspora (scattering) began. The exile saw the destruction of Jerusalem as well as large groups of Jews in Babylon, Palestine and Egypt, and soon they would spread throughout the known world, a situation that continues until the present day.

The people of God should not have been surprised by this course of events. After all, they were warned already that their sin would lead to judgment. It was built into the very fabric of the covenant that Israel enjoyed with God beginning with Moses. After giving the law, God also enumerated blessings for obedience but also punishments for disobedience (Deuteronomy 27–28), many of which anticipated the exile (see, for example, Deuteronomy 28:49-52).

Though the people of God now experienced the heavy hand of judgment, God was not yet done with them. As the prophets had foreseen (see study 16), restoration would follow judgment. Indeed, the very end of 2 Kings, written during the exile, gives a hint at good things to come. The

last event mentioned is the release of King Jehoiachin (2 Kings 25:27-30), the king who was exiled in 597 B.C., from a Babylonian prison during the reign of the Babylonian king Awel-Marduk (562–560 B.C.).

As we turn now to the period following the exile, we will see that God indeed brings a remnant back to Judah, though many will stay in the Diaspora, scattered in foreign nations. Our primary sources for learning about this period of time are Ezra–Nehemiah (originally one, not two books) and Esther. The first informs us about events in Palestine, and the second gives us a picture of the Diaspora.

Ezra 1–6 informs us about the early return from exile, beginning with the Cyrus decree. As we examine the events of the postexilic period, we are amazed right from the start how God used the political and military strategies of foreign people to further his plans. In 539 B.C., Persia, under King Cyrus the Great, defeated Babylon and in this way inherited Babylon's empire, including the province of Yehud (Judah). One of the first things Cyrus did was to allow the Jews to begin to return to their homeland and to rebuild the temple.

We know from other ancient Near Eastern documents of this time period that the Jews were not the object of special attention from Cyrus. Rather, Cyrus allowed all of Babylon's vassal people who had been exiled to return to their countries and rebuild their temples. While Cyrus was just implementing a different political strategy for controlling subjugated states, God used this for his own good purposes, a theme that we will see throughout this time period.

The first to heed the call and lead groups back to the land were Sheshbazzar and Zerubbabel, the latter a descendant of David and the appointed governor of the now Persian province of Yehud (Judah). Cyrus even allowed them to take back the sacred objects that the Babylonians had plundered from the temple. Indeed, they were specifically commissioned to rebuild the temple, and they built the sacrificial altar and laid the foundation for that critical building right away (Ezra 3). However, they soon ran into opposition (Ezra 4:1-5) and other distractions, so they stopped working on the temple for a while. However, after a period of time, God sent his prophets, Zechariah and Haggai (Ezra 5:1-2; see also the prophetic books Haggai and Zechariah) to exhort them to finish the building in spite of opposition. The people under the leadership of Zerubbabel responded positively, and the temple was completed in 515 B.C. This temple was the one that Jesus would visit during his life (though greatly expanded by Herod the Great).

Ezra 7 begins the account of the period of the great leaders Ezra and Nehemiah. There is a considerable time gap between Ezra 6 and 7. The first six chapters of the book cover the time period from 539 until 515 B.C. Ezra's return takes place in the seventh year of King Artaxerxes (I), which would be 458 B.C. We know little about what happened in the meantime in Yehud, but now we see another Persian king en-couraging a Jewish leader to return home. The Persian king urged Ezra to restore the law in the land. Again, the Persian king has Persian interests in mind. They had a far-flung empire, and unlike some imperialist nations who try to impose their law on all the people, they ruled largely through en-couraging local governments like Judah to use their own law code to keep order in their society. Like with Cyrus's earlier pol-icy that resulted in some Jews returning to their homeland, so Artaxerxes' policy was used by God to restore the ancient law of Moses among his people.

Some years later the same Persian king, Artaxerxes, allowed Nehemiah to return to Judah. While Ezra was a priest and scholar and the perfect one to restore the law, Nehe-miah was a political figure. God used him to restore the defensive wall of Jerusalem.

The story begins when Nehemiah was serving as a cupbearer to the king back in the royal city of Susa. Now a cupbearer was not a mere servant bringing the king drinks. The position was that of an impor-tant adviser and confidant of the king. One day Nehemiah's brother came from Jerusalem and gave him a dire report con-cerning the condition of the city. The next day Nehemiah had his worry written all over his face, and the king asked him what made him so concerned. When Nehemiah told him about Jerusalem, the king then appointed him governor of the province with the commission to restore the city and its wall.

Again, God used the self-interest of the Persian Empire for his own purposes. At this time, the Persians were most concerned about the Greeks, their main military rival. To defend against the Greeks, the Persians wanted their border provinces not only to be peaceful and content, but also defended against attack. A loyal native governor like Nehemiah, who would rebuild the city's defenses, fit perfectly into Persian needs at the moment. Again, God used Persian self-interest in order to accomplish his purpose of restoring his people to the land.

While the Persians supported Nehemiah's mission, local non-Jewish officials certainly did not, and they did their best to undermine the rebuilding of the wall. Nehemiah had to be on his guard constantly against these enemies, and it took real courage to build the wall in a relatively short time.

But the Jews, with God's help, did build the walls, and by the end of the book of Ezra-Nehemiah, the temple is restored, the law reestablished and the wall rebuilt. After these three momentous events, Ezra and Nehemiah together led the people in a renewal of their covenant with God (see Nehemiah 8–12). What a magnificent and triumphant conclusion to the account of the events of the postexilic period! The only problem is—there is one more chapter in the book, and it is a strange one.

Nehemiah 13 is part of Nehemiah's memoir. After his thirteen-year tour of duty as governor of Yehud, he had gone back to Persia for a period of time, but now he has just returned. And what did he find

when he got back? Trouble! Nehemiah lists all the problems and the sins of the people and the priests. There were pagan foreigners that were in the assembly of God, people were using the sacred precincts of the temple for profane purposes, the sabbath was not observed, and on and on. Nehemiah took stern measures to confront those who were sinning in this way, but the message of the book is clear. The restoration has begun, but it is anything but complete. We will return to this theme later when we look at the book from a New Testament perspective.

But before we look at the New Testament, we turn our attention to the book of Esther. While Ezra-Nehemiah gives us a window on the restoration of the Jews to the Holy Land, Esther concerns Jews who choose to remain in the Diaspora. Is God with these people even though they don't return?

Esther is most notable for being one of two books in the Old Testament (the other is the Song of Songs) that never mentions God. However, as we will see, God makes his presence known very clearly in the remarkable reversals in the story. As we look at the plot of Esther, we will pay close attention to these reversals, and we will also observe how "feasts" play a central role as setting in the book. Both these features of Esther point to the message the book is imparting to us the readers.

As a matter of fact, the book begins with a feast, a huge feast thrown by the Persian king Xerxes (also known as Ahasuerus). Xerxes was the Persian king who ruled between 485 and 465 B.C., thus placing this story between that of Sheshbazzar and Zerubbabel (539–515 B.C.) and Ezra and Nehemiah (458–c. 430 B.C.). All the action of Esther takes place in Persia.

This feast lasted many days and involved all the leading military and political officials of Xerxes' reign. We are not told the purpose of this feast, but we have a good idea why he threw this lavish party. We know from extrabiblical sources (the Greek historian Herodotus) that Xerxes threw a big banquet in anticipation of his invasion of Greece. If this connection is correct, then the purpose of this feast was similar to a pep rally, showing the power and wealth of the empire in order to instill confidence for the upcoming war and in particular establishing Xerxes' power and authority.

Thus, we can imagine the problem that arose when his queen, Vashti (who herself was giving a banquet [Esther 1:9]), refused to appear at his command to display her beauty before the feasting nobles and generals. From his vantage point the king had no choice but to depose her, thus creating an opening for a new queen.

But how to choose a new queen? His advisers recommend what is essentially a contest. All the beautiful young women would be gathered and prepared for a one-night liaison with the king. Among these women, Esther was chosen.

When Esther first appears in the book, she is introduced along with her cousin, who was in charge of her, Mordecai (Esther 2:2-7). We learn about Mordecai's background, though its significance won't be revealed till later. At this point we should just remember he is "son of Jair, the son of Shimei, the son of Kish" (Esther 2:5). About Esther, we learn she "had a lovely figure and was beautiful" (v. 7), so we are not surprised later when the king chooses Esther to be his new queen.

Next we are introduced to Haman, the last major character in the book, when Xerxes gives him "a seat of honor higher than that of all the other nobles" (Esther 3:1). We are also told about his background. He is the "son of Hammedatha, the Agagite," a fact that also has great significance, which I will explain shortly. For now, I will just point out that Mordecai's and Haman's backgrounds go a long way toward explaining why they hate each other. Mordecai refuses to show Haman respect, and Haman determines not just to kill Mordecai but all of his people, the Jews.

To effect his plan, Haman gets Xerxes to agree to exterminate the Jews by raising suspicion about their loyalty and offering large sums of money. They choose a date by casting lots (*purim*, see later) and determine to allow Haman and his people to exterminate the Jews in about a year's time.

Mordecai, who as we have seen has a talent at discovering secret plots, finds out about Haman and Xerxes' deal. He knows he cannot do anything, so he approaches his cousin Esther, who at first is extremely hesitant to bring this matter to the attention of the king. Finally, Mordecai reminds her that not even her high position will save her from death if Haman's plan goes through, so she decides to act. Mordecai's persuasive words are the most memorable in the book, "And who knows but that you have come to your royal position for such a time as this?" (Esther 4:14).

Esther's hesitation arose because not even she could approach the king uninvited. If she did, she risked her life unless he held out his golden scepter to her to enter. To her relief, he gladly admitted her into his presence, and she used her moment to invite him to a feast along with Haman. At his feast, she invited them to another feast on the next day.

At this point the narrator turns attention to Haman, who is beside himself with pride and joy. As the recipient of the attention of the king and the queen, he believes himself to be highly exalted. There was still one nagging problem—Mordecai!

When Haman expressed his hatred for Mordecai and his friends, Haman's friends urged him to simply kill him, and in response Haman had a seventy-five-foot pole set up to impale him. Things were looking good for Haman and very bad for Mordecai and his people, but events were about to reverse this outlook.

That night the king had insomnia, and he told his attendants to read to him from his royal annals. They "just so happened" (but we all know this is no coincidence) to read about the time that Mordecai foiled the assassination plot. The king then discovered that nothing had been done to honor this man who saved his life. So the next morning when his highest official ar-

rived in court he asked, "What should be done for the man the king delights to honor?" (Esther 6:6). Haman, of course, thinks it is him, so he suggests the highest possible honor, to have the person mounted on the king's horse and draped in the royal robe with an attendant leading the horse proclaiming, "This is what is done for the man the king delights to honor!" (Esther 6:9).

Imagine Haman's shock and dismay when the king told him to do this for his hated enemy Mordecai! But do it he did, and afterward when he told his wife, she told him to prepare for his downfall.

And the downfall comes fast and furious. When he attended the second feast Esther prepared for him, she accuses him of secretly plotting to kill her and her people. The king is so upset he leaves the room only to return to Haman falling over the queen begging her to help him. At his attendants' advice, the king orders that Haman be impaled on the pole that he built to impale Mordecai, another drastic reversal.

Still, there is the problem of the decree that allows the enemies of the Jews, Haman's people, to annihilate them, and in Persia a king could not reverse his decree. However, that does not stop him from issuing a second decree that allows the Jews to arm themselves and attack their enemies, and when this happens, the Jews completely destroy them. So the day appointed for the destruction of the Jews is the day the Jews destroy their enemies, another reversal. By now, we are thoroughly aware that these events are not coincidental at all, but behind them is the secret providence of God, protecting his people, even though they do not live in the Promised Land. He will even take care of them in the Diaspora.

But now let us return to the genealogy of Mordecai and Haman. There is more to the animosity between them and more to the conflict between the Jews and Haman's people than meets the eye. At least the modern eye—right from the start the original readers would have known what is going on. They would have known that Mordecai, as a descendant of Jair, Kish and Shimei, was also a descendant of King Saul. And they would also know that an Agagite was an Amalekite.

The hostility between the Amalekites and Israel goes back to Exodus 17:8-16. As Israel departed from Egypt, the Amalekites picked off the stragglers until Israel defeated them. This battle is well known as the time that Moses raised his rod, signifying God's presence, to assure the victory. At this time God decreed, "Because hands were lifted up against the throne of the LORD, the LORD will be at war against the Amalekites from generation to generation" (Exodus 17:16), a decree that was reaffirmed in the Mosaic law (Deuteronomy 25:17-19). Saul enters the picture because he had the opportunity to follow through on this divine command as he defeated the Amalekites and their king Agag, but he fails to do so (1 Samuel 15), angering the prophet Samuel. But now many centuries later, God uses these events in the Persian Empire to finish unfinished business.

The Jewish people survived; their enemies were destroyed. Mordecai assumed the position that was occupied by Haman. How was this celebrated? By a great feast, Purim, a feast celebrated annually by Jewish people up to the present day!

Thus, while the exile was the judgment of God against his people because of their sin, it was not the end of the story. God restored his people in the land, as we learn about in Ezra-Nehemiah, and he continues to be with his people in the Diaspora, as we learn in the book of Esther. With these books we come to the end of the story of God's people in the Old Testament. The Christian reader knows that great things are yet to come.

Reading Study Guide

1. The temple was God's dwelling on earth. How could God allow it to be destroyed?

2. Who did Nebuchadnezzar exile to Babylon, and who did he allow to remain behind?

What happened to those who stayed in Judah?

3. What are the role and the significance of Gedaliah in the aftermath of the destruction of Jerusalem?

4. What significance do the curses of the covenant have to do with the destruction of Jerusalem?

5. What role does the Persian government play in the restoration of the Jews to Judah?

6. Summarize the role and accomplishments of the following: Sheshbazzar and Zerubbabel, Ezra and Nehemiah, Mordecai and Esther.

7. Why doesn't the book of Esther ever refer to God by name?

Even so, does God have a role in the book?

8. Explain why Haman and Mordecai hate each other.

Anticipating the New Testament

With the exile and the restoration we come to the end of Old Testament history. As we have seen, the return of some of the exiles to Jerusalem indicated that God was not done with his people. However, as Nehemiah 13 indicated, much work still needed to be done. In addition, the people of God, though back in the land, were not politically independent. There was no Davidic king on the throne; they were living under the control of the Persians.

In the covenant with David, God had said, "your house and your kingdom will endure forever before me; your throne will be established forever" (2 Samuel 7:16).

1. If so, why was Zedekiah the last descendant of David to occupy the throne in Jerusalem?

2. How does the New Testament resolve this issue?

In the Reading we saw that Nehemiah 13 concluded the story of the postexilic period in Judah on a depressing note. It appears that while God allowed the Jews to return to Jerusalem, there was plenty of work yet to do; the full promise of God had not been realized.

3. How does the book of Nehemiah then anticipate the events of the New Testament?

The book of Esther narrates a close call for the people of God. The focus is on the people who still remained scattered even after the return of some Jewish people to Jerusalem (the Diaspora). But they almost all, both those in and out of the land, would have been killed by their enemies if Haman had had his way.

4. What would have happened to the promise of a Messiah if Haman had succeeded?

The Ancient Story and Our Story

The story of the exile and the restoration illustrates two fundamental realities in our relationship with God. The first lesson taught by the exile is that God hates sin and will judge it. He may not do so right away, but judgment is inevitable. God told Moses that he "does not leave the guilty unpunished" (Exodus 34:7). This statement is as true today as it was at the time of Moses.

The second lesson taught by the restoration is that God is merciful and forgiving. God also told Moses that he was "the compassionate and gracious God, slow to anger, abounding in love and faithfulness, maintaining love to thousands, and forgiving wickedness, rebellion and sin" (Exodus 34:6-7). In other words, our sin does not consign us unalterably to God's judgment, but if we repent, then he forgives and restores our relationship, thanks to Jesus Christ's death and resurrection. We should remember as well that repentance is not a one-time affair. After we become Christians, we continue to struggle with sin; thus we repent daily.

Looking Ahead

With this chapter, we have come to the end of our study of the Old Testament. We have moved from the account of creation and Fall, the patriarchs (Abraham, Isaac and Jacob) and Joseph, the exodus and wilderness wanderings, the conquest, and the period of the judges. We continued with a look at the rise of the monarchy, its sad division into a northern and southern kingdom, and then finally the exile and restoration. Besides the books that present the history of God's people, we also looked at the law, wisdom literature, the psalms and the prophets, as well as Israel's worship institutions (tabernacle/temple, priests and sacrifices). After the Old Testament comes to a close, we enter into a period known as the Intertestamental Period before the opening of the New Testament. But that is a subject for another book.

Going Deeper

Jobes, Karen. *Esther.* NIV Application Commentary. Grand Rapids: Zondervan, 1999.

Throntveit, Mark A. *Ezra-Nehemiah.* Interpretation. Louisville, KY: Westminster John Knox, 1992.

Discipleship Essentials
Greg Ogden
978-0-8308-1087-1, paperback, 237 pages

Leadership Essentials
Greg Ogden and Daniel Meyer
978-0-8308-1097-0, paperback, 176 pages

Witness Essentials
Daniel Meyer
978-0-8308-1089-5, paperback, 208 pages

The Essential Commandment
Greg Ogden
978-0-8308-1088-8, paperback, 204 pages

Coming in Fall 2014
New Testament Essentials
Robbie Fox Castleman
978-0-8308-1052-9, paperback